THE HOME UNIVERSITY LIBRARY
OF MODERN KNOWLEDGE

237

SCOTLAND
PAST AND PRESENT

EDITOR OF
The Home University Library
of Modern Knowledge

SIR GEORGE CLARK, D.LITT., F.B.A.

Scotland
Past and Present

J. M. REID

LONDON
OXFORD UNIVERSITY PRESS
NEW YORK TORONTO
1959

Oxford University Press, Amen House, London E.C.4

GLASGOW NEW YORK TORONTO MELBOURNE WELLINGTON
BOMBAY CALCUTTA MADRAS KARACHI KUALA LUMPUR
CAPE TOWN IBADAN NAIROBI ACCRA

Printed in Great Britain

TO MY WIFE

CONTENTS

A MAP OF SCOTLAND, ILLUSTRATING REFERENCES
IN THE TEXT, APPEARS ON PP. 20–1.

ACKNOWLEDGEMENTS

THE Author's thanks are due to all who have given him help and advice, among them Sir John Spencer Muirhead, Professor A. D. Gibb, Dr. John Highet, Mr. W. S. Robertson, Mr. Alex. F. Yeaman, and, notably, Sir George Clark, whose editorial guidance has been both useful and stimulating.

But for the assistance of his daughter Jean this book could never have struggled into type.

Responsibility for the opinions expressed here is, of course, exclusively his own.

PROLOGUE

SCOTLAND, the subject of this book is not too easily defined. Certainly the country can be identified in any atlas. Its boundaries have been unaltered for four centuries. But what they contain is something unusual, perhaps unique, in the world of the Twentieth Century.

Scotland is not a state either in the European sense of the word or in the American one. It has no autonomous government. It is not, and, in its present circumstances could not be, a member of the United Nations. It is not a unit of a federal system like one of the American states, the Canadian provinces or the Swiss cantons. On the other hand, it is not, in any ordinary sense, an area of local government. It is not one county of the United Kingdom but thirty-three—more or less, according to the rather uncertain modern reckoning of such things. On the other hand it is quite unlike those English 'regions', the West Country, the Midlands, which can be recognized in a general way but are seldom very sharply delineated. No one will argue whether a particular piece of country is Scottish or not.[1]

Perhaps one can meet this difficulty most exactly by saying that Scotland is that part of the island of Great Britain, mainly north of latitude 55, where certain

[1] Many Scotsmen think that Berwick-on-Tweed, now attached to Northumberland, should again be the county town of Berwickshire, but there is no uncertainty about the present Border line.

peculiar conditions prevail. It is subject, for instance, to a system of law distinct from England's and, indeed, different in its origin and broad principles from the law of all other English-speaking countries. North of its Border the established church is Presbyterian, bishops are dissenters, the State has no control over the Church's government or the choice of its leading officials. Many departments of administration which in England and Wales come under different Ministers, are controlled in Scotland by one member of the British Cabinet. Scottish education has an organization and tradition of its own. Scottish local government has its own forms and names: the towns are burghs, the mayors are provosts, the chairmen of county councils are conveners of their counties. Heraldry is ruled by the Lord Lyon King of Arms and his Lyon Court, not by the English Earl Marshal and his College of Heralds in London. Football and other sports are controlled in Scotland by Scottish bodies whose teams take part in international matches.

No doubt these things are no more than the shell of Scottish life, but they are facts about it which are most easily set down and least subject to varying opinions. What is behind the shell? It is not a kingdom, though this word is sometimes used of Scotland still. The Kingdom of Scotland, like the Kingdom of England, disappeared two and a half centuries ago, when the Union of the two countries' Parliaments followed the Union of Crowns, which had brought a Scots King to London in 1603. Scotland's only organ of political self-government is the Parliament of the United Kingdom, a Parliament in which the Scots, unlike the English, can never hope to have a majority of their own representatives. In this sense the situation of Scots is quite different from that of Englishmen to whom the United Kingdom must often seem a mere extension of their own country.

Can one say, then, that the thing behind the shell is a nation? Undoubtedly it was a nation which secreted this shell—the National Church, the laws, the forms of administration that make a separate Scottish Department of State seem convenient or necessary are the outgrowth of long ages of national history. To the modern observer they may seem mere relics of the past: if that were a true opinion they would not be likely to last much longer, however picturesquely they may break the increasingly uniform surface of the British scene. There is no doubt, however, that most Scottish people are still inclined to think of themselves as a nation, at least from some points of view. They will tack the word 'national' on to the names of respected institutions or ambitious commercial companies. Lord Balfour's Royal Commission on Scottish Affairs, which was certainly in no sense a politically Nationalist body and was inclined to feel that most things in Scotland were moving in the right direction, insisted in its report (1954) that 'the recognition of Scotland's national status' by British Ministers was necessary to the smooth and efficient working of government.

Scotland, then, is evidently a nation in some sense. A nation which, for 250 years, has kept its individuality without the political framework of a State to support it is a very unusual thing in the modern world. This was not so when the Union between England and Scotland was made. Then European states were not in principle national. Political boundaries cut easily through regions which language, race and tradition might have united, or bound together national groups which had not much in common except their loyalty to one king or government. In our own day we have seen the collapse of most multi-national states. In modern Britain both Englishmen and Scotsmen now call themselves British, at least in certain moods and on certain occasions. Yet the smaller of these peoples still calls itself Scottish too. A country so far apart from the ordinary rules of modern societies as this one is surely worth some attention.

Chapter One

A VIEW OF SCOTLAND

As it tapers from south to north, the island of Great Britain is repeatedly nipped by its seas. It narrows first between the Bristol Channel on the west and the Thames estuary on the east, then between the Mersey and the Humber, then where the deep wedge of the Solway Firth presses in from the Irish Sea, then between two wide estuaries, the Firths of Clyde and Forth, then between the Firth of Lorne, reaching northeast from the Atlantic and the great bay of the Moray Firth, which belongs to the North Sea. These waters sketch a division of the island into seven blocks. Four are South England, the English Midlands and East Anglia, Wales, and North England. The three northern ones are Scotland, so cut about that there is scarcely a habitable spot in the country more than forty miles from the tide.

It is separated from England chiefly by moorlands and the sea. From the south one comes over high, barren country to the rivers which, for a few miles, mark the Border—the Tweed on the east, the Sark and Liddell on the west. These streams themselves have never been much of an obstacle to travel: indeed the main roads to Scotland pass over them. It is the Solway Firth and the broad, though not dramatic, waste of the Cheviot Hills which made a frontier there. The fertile

English lowland narrows and disappears among the rocks of the Northumberland coast. On the west it ends with the streams that run down to Lancashire. North of this moorland emptiness the first Scottish valleys are planted and peopled. But they are not large, and between them the high-lying country reaches north again, expanding and filling most of the southern block of Scotland, which stretches from the Solway to the Firths of Forth and Clyde.

Oddly enough, this region, consisting mainly of green hills, moors and the valleys between them, is sometimes called the Lowlands. Most of its people are certainly Lowlanders, in any sense, including the quite special one that, unlike the Scots Highlanders, very few of them have spoken a Celtic language for at least five centuries past. But the true lowlands where population has always been thickest, are narrow plains—in Dumfriesshire, just north of the Border, in the seaward parts of Galloway, along the curve of the Ayrshire coast. These are on the west. On the east there is the valley of the Tweed and the wider coastal plain of Lothian, almost cut in two by the Pentland Hills, Edinburgh rock and Arthur's Seat. Each of these is separated from the others by some mass of hills, and it is only at the isthmus between Forth and Clyde that the Lothian plain flows west to meet the lowlands of Lanarkshire and Renfrewshire. The lowland flows northward too, narrowing to a few fields' breadth as it passes the rock of Stirling and broken by groups of hills—the Kilpatricks, the Campsies, the Ochils, the Sidlaws. It swells into the valley of Menteith on one side and the peninsula of Fife on the other. Another strip of upland separates these from Strathearn, and then the little plains run north and east—Strathtay, Strathmore, the Howe o' the Mearns, the Carse of Gowrie, the Angus coast lands sloping to the sea. There is a break of moorish upland just south of Aberdeen, then the sea plain widens again in Formartine and Buchan and swings west along the Moray Firth, richer but narrowing till it reaches the second Scottish isthmus, sixty miles wide, and the Great Glen. North of that is the lowland of Easter Ross, breaking against the mountains, and the northmost mainland county, Caithness, partly a lowland too, though, like everything north and south-west of the Moray coast-land, it is reckoned to belong to the Highland region.

Not one of these little plains is much more than ten miles across, between uncultivable hill and hill, or hill and sea. Facing all of them north of Forth and Clyde is the wall of the Highlands, mountains not high by Continental standards (anything over 3,000 feet is recognized as remarkable, a 'Munro') but dramatic, usually close-set, and inhospitable. Mountains, moors and lochs fill the greater part of the two northern blocks of Scottish mainland, on either side of the Great Glen. It is possible, no doubt, to arrange the mountains in groups or ranges—the Archean peaks of the north-west, the Grampians and Cairngorms of the central Highlands, running towards the North Sea, Drumalban (the 'Backbone of Scotland') reaching from the Clyde to the Great Glen—but the form of the Highland country is given to it mainly by the river valleys and volcanic faults. In the west the valleys are drowned and form sea-lochs that reach deep among the hills, so that the West Coast from the Clyde northwards is a fringe of rocky peninsulas. Beyond it is another fringe of islands, the Inner Hebrides, lying close to the mainland shores or reaching towards Ireland, and the Outer Hebrides, the Long Island, thirty miles out, or more, across the stormy Minches. On a small scale this side of Scotland recalls the Norwegian fjords and *skjaergaard*. North of the mainland are the two far-stretching island groups of Orkney and Shetland, which in their history and tradition are almost as much Norse as Scottish. And directly west of the Clyde, linked to the rest of the peopled country only by sea and mountain passes, is the milder, more fruitful Highland region of Argyllshire, where the first Scottish kingdom was planted.

Historically, Scotland is one of the smaller European countries. It is not, however, one of the smallest. Its area is roughly twice Denmark's and three times Belgium's, and the shape of its 30,000 square miles, scattered over a great background of sea, makes them seem wider than they are. From the northernmost Shetland isles to the Mull of Galloway in the south, roughly 450 miles, is almost as far as from the western Border to Paris. Practically such distances have been, and sometimes still are, even more formidable than they look. The train journey from Edinburgh to the north coast at Thurso can be almost twice as long in time as the run to London. The journey by train and steamer from Glasgow to Stornoway, the one town in the Outer Hebrides, takes thirteen hours. Flight has brought some of the remoter places much nearer in time, but it is still true, as it has always been, that the fringes of Scotland can be as far from one another as Paris is from Poland. More important, historically, than this remoteness of the outer corners of the country has been the fact that there is no large fertile plain from which a centralized state could easily expand itself. The lowlands, as we have seen, are long, thin and broken, and though in the past century and a half, three-quarters of the Scottish population has concentrated itself between the coasts of the Firth of Clyde and those of the Tay, no one city has ever dominated Scotland as London, Paris and Copenhagen dominate England, France and Denmark.

When one remembers this physical framework the history of Scotland is, in some senses, a surprising record of union. The group of British tribes who are called Caledonians held together remarkably well against the Romans. The Pictish kingdom which took their place was the largest political unit in the Britain of the Dark Ages, stretching from Orkney (perhaps Shetland) to the Firth of Forth. The victory of one of its rulers, Brude mac Bili, over the most powerful of the early English kingdoms, Northumbria, in 685, made the growth of an independent Scotland possible.

There were other little kingdoms beside Pictland— Dalriada (Argyllshire), a colony of Gaelic-speaking Scots from Ireland; British Strathclyde, where some of the oldest Welsh poems seem to have been composed; Anglic Bernicia in what are now the Lothians, Berwickshire and Northumberland. But when the Scots, backed by the prestige of the missionary church which the

Irishman, St. Columba, had founded in Iona, became
the rulers of Pictland, where their language had spread
before them, this united kingdom withstood the Viking
raids and invasions more successfully than England or
Ireland. The Norsemen took the Isles, setting up a
powerful earldom in Orkney and little kingdoms in the
West, but the mass of Scotland never fell to them. No
doubt the poverty and difficulty of the hill country was
a sort of safeguard against the ambition of conquering
chiefs, but the Picts had evolved a Christian civilization
of their own which seems to have survived their
language. One sees something of it in the remarkable
carved stones, at once stylized and lively, that show us
mounted warriors, priests, huntsmen (as well as symbols
that are still mysteries) and seem to foreshadow the
life of the High Middle Ages, as those strange double-
walled towers, the brochs, which must have been rising
round the Pictish coasts before the Roman Empire fell,
foreshadow the medieval castle.

When a Danish king was ruling England, Scotland
fixed its Border on the Tweed and even took its present
name. The Anglic south-west was conquered. The last
king of Strathclyde, where Gaelic was probably already
driving out Welsh, was succeeded by the Scottish king's
heir. To complete itself Scotland had to regain the
islands which had once been Pictish or Dalriadic, and
this was done, by degrees, over the next four and a half
centuries.

Before the process was completed by the recovery of
Orkney, however, Scottish unity had been affirmed in
the most dramatic way possible. Scotsmen of all

classes and kinds, not merely the lords and levies who normally made up medieval armies, had shown that they could combine to defend the country's independence. No doubt some of the marks of national feeling can be found elsewhere towards the end of the Thirteenth Century. But there is a real sense in which the Scots were the first people to act as a nation in our sense of the word.

Shortly after Edward I of England began his attempt to conquer and occupy Scotland by force of arms in 1296 the Scots found themselves without a king. On the face of things their society was far from being united: certainly it was very far from uniformity. There was no one national language. Many of the feudal lords were Anglo-Normans. A sort of English speech had been spreading over the Lowlands for two centuries from the original Anglic corner south of the Forth. The North and West spoke Gaelic. Organized feudal law and administration had also spread over districts once tribal or Scandinavian in their way of life, but its roots were not very deep. The little towns, the monasteries and dioceses had only a few generations of organized life behind them. But in a quarter of a century's struggle the clergy, townsmen, peasants, great Norse-Gaelic chieftains of the West, and a determining number of lords and knights came together. Two great soldiers— the knight William Wallace, who organized armies of infantry in that age of horsemen, and Robert Bruce, the new king—led this resistance to a power enormously greater and richer than their own. Towards the end of this story the Scots leaders approved at Arbroath that letter to the Pope which remains, for their country, what Magna Carta is in the tradition of England:

'From these innumerable evils, with the help of Him who healeth after wounds, we have been delivered by our most valiant prince and king, Lord Robert; who, that he might free his people and heritage from the hands of their enemies rose like another Maccabeus or Joshua, cheerfully enduring toil and weariness, hunger and peril. . . . But if he were to abandon this task, wishing to subject us or our realm to the King of England or the English, we should instantly set ourselves to expel him as the betrayer of his own rights and ours, and would make a new King who would be capable of our defence. For so long as one hundred men of us remain we shall never submit under any conditions to the domination of the English. It is not for glory, riches or honours that we fight, but only for freedom, which no good man will abandon but with his life.'

So much for the unity which history and human will imposed so early on a framework of physical division. But the effects of this physical framework have been none the less deep. They made Scotland, in the past, a country of small and rather isolated communities. When the advance of royal administration on patterns borrowed from feudal England or Normandy was checked by the confusion of the long Wars of Independence, the Celtic, tribal ways of life revived in the Highlands. The clans came into being. Each district or group of glens was something between a little kingdom and a large family. The chief ruled, usually with councillors who were the leading cadets of his house. He made wars and alliances with his neighbours. Most

of his people took his family name and believed themselves to be related to him: in the course of centuries
this belief was probably justified. And though clans, in
the proper sense, belonged to the Highlands, the same
sort of spirit spread though the whole country.

Lords who were, unquestionably, the descendants of
Anglo-Norman knights deliberately planted on their
lands by the great, feudalizing, King David I, in the
Twelfth Century, came to be recognized as the Heads
of Names, every other holder of which owed them a
certain loyalty. They drew their legal rights from their
baronies or from their position as hereditary sheriffs of
counties—for even royal offices of this sort became
hereditary. But the actual power of the baron who was
Head of a Name might be far greater than his formal
ones and reach well beyond the lands which belonged
to him in law.

This national pleasure in the idea of clanship has
shown itself rather amusingly even in the last century
and a half. Tartan, the sort of chequered cloth which,
from time to time sweeps the world of fashion, had
undoubtedly been worn by the Gaels for many centuries before it was forbidden under the Disarming
Act after the last Jacobite rebellion, but it is very
doubtful indeed whether many (if any) of the setts now
recognized as belonging to particular clans had been
appropriated in that way before 1745. After the Highland dress was legalized again in 1782, however, a whole
series of clan tartans, each carefully distinguished from
the other, began to come into being. When George IV
visited Edinburgh in 1822—the first king to come to

Scotland since Charles II—the city was filled with kilted chiefs and their followers. In no time Lowland families whose ancestors might have been horrified by the idea of being mistaken for Gaels were claiming tartans of their own. There soon were (and there still are) Douglas, Hamilton, Scott, Home tartans, each to be worn only by people who can claim relationship with these families.

In old Scotland this family feeling touched the Throne itself, especially after the Bruces were succeeded by the Stewarts, who were soon related by marriage to most of the great noble houses in Scotland. The king was felt to be at once the father of his country and (in a very vague way) every man's cousin.

All this gives an anarchic air to much of Scottish history. There were innumerable feuds and little wars, the less avoidable because the Crown was weakened by a long succession of minorities. But the sense of family, of personal relationships overshadowing legal ones, also gave the nation a peculiar sort of elasticity and even strength. In a crisis which seemed to touch the country's existence, men would come together not simply at the command of the king's ministers but in a body, or a group of bodies, moved by feeling. Sentiment and a diffused popular will, not centralized power, are the determining things in the great movements of the Scottish past.

Without these things the long struggle for national freedom, waged at times with the merest sketch of a political organization behind it, could not have been maintained; the tremendous overturn of the Reformation, carried out not by the Government (as in most Protestant countries) but against it, would scarcely have been possible: the improbable, strictly unreasonable, adventure of the Covenanting Wars, which sought to impose the Scottish form of Protestantism on England and Ireland, could never have been attempted and certainly would not have left behind it, in its failure, a sense of national commitment which lasted for generations. It is not to be pretended that the Scottish people were unanimous in any of these efforts, even the first: simply that there was, in each case, a determining will which moved not a small group of governors only but people of all classes. This showed itself again after the collapse of the Covenant in a passionate pursuit of new wealth, in the effort to found a Scottish trading empire overseas, ending with the shattering failure of Darien; then, after the Parliamentary Union with England, in the gospel of Adam Smith, the sudden growth of trade, industries and banks, the re-shaping of the countryside, the mushroom creation of great cities and new towns which filled the second half of the Eighteenth Century and all of the Nineteenth.

None of these movements was planned or directed by the established rulers of the country. All of them came out of the nation, out of a people which could be roused but could not be commanded, partly because of that intense feeling for freedom which breathes in the Declaration of Arbroath, partly because of the splitting and localization of authority which the physical structure of the country favoured. Certainly a price had to be paid for the frequent weakness of the central government.

Though Scotland had all the organs of a European state—law courts, parliament, chancery, treasury, admiralty and the rest—half of the country stood outside this system from the late Middle Ages till the mid-Eighteenth Century.

It is wrong to say that the Highlands were not Scottish in feeling, still more mistaken to suggest that the Lowlanders were almost English and only the Highlanders true heirs of the past, because they spoke Gaelic. The division between the two halves of Scotland was strictly a domestic thing, but there was a real chasm, not only in language but in thought, ambitions, habits, even food and dress, often religion, between the feudal or post-feudal south and east and the tribal northern, western glens and islands. The Lowlands were essentially a part of evolving Western Europe, the Highlands had had one foot in that world, the other in the sort of life that was lived among the Celtic peoples before the Romans came. Yet this cleavage seemed so much a part of the nature of Scotland itself and the old Highland way of life so essential a strand in the national one that the events which brought it to an end have often been treated as the last chapter of Scottish history. Very little in the national consciousness of the country was changed by the Union of the Crowns in 1603, when the King of Scots became King of England too. Even the Union of the Parliaments of England and Scotland in 1707 made a less dramatic breach with the past than the defeat of the Jacobite rising of 1745-6.

The Forty-five has held a peculiar place in the

memories of Scotsmen. In itself it was a mere adventure, an episode in a European war, though its leader, Prince Charles Edward, was a romantic and endearing figure and the very rashness of the enterprise which took him from Moidart to Derby (and might, just conceivably, have carried him to London) gave it a sort of sunset glory. Very few Lowlanders and only one group among clan chiefs were ready to fight for Bonnie Prince Charlie, but after his failure whole generations of Scots were willing to sing about him. Though the Stewarts had ceased to be possible leaders of a united Protestant Scotland, 'No Union' was inscribed on Jacobite sword-blades—the only swords to be drawn in that century for the idea of Scottish nationhood. Till our own day, when a new form of the national idea has begun to take shape, most poets and novelists (perhaps most Scotsmen) have been Jacobite at heart in their backward-looking moments.

For Highlanders this persistent Jacobite sentiment has had a special meaning. The clans, whether they had fought for Prince Charlie or not, never recovered from the effects of his disaster at Culloden, which broke them, both militarily and as social units. Yet in social atmosphere the two regions, Highland and Lowland, always had a great deal in common. In both parts of Scotland there was a deep sense of aristocracy, of the rights and privileges of family. But there was also a special sort of equality, an egalitarianism not of wealth or rights, but of pride. Every Campbell was, after all, a Campbell, every Kerr a Kerr, and every Scot had a son's place in Scotland.

In certain moods Scotsmen were, and still are, 'a' Jock Tamson's bairns', the children of the same home. Even in the Twentieth Century this has endowed Scottish people with a very particular sort of democratic feeling which has sometimes been assertive enough but yet can leave room for a possibly anachronistic respect for rank and distinction, provided that the title or achievement to be respected also belongs to the Scottish family. The sense of personal relationship between very diverse and independent individuals and groups has had a softening, moderating influence on Scottish life which is, perhaps, not too easily seen on the surface of history.

The story of Scotland sometimes seems almost extravagantly full of violence: there are occasional spectacular atrocities like the massacre of Royalist prisoners and camp-followers after Philiphaugh and at Dunaverty, or the burning of the Mackenzies at Kilchrist. But there are no social wars or jacqueries, no St. Bartholomews, nothing to equal the vengeful slaughter that followed an English rising like the Pilgrimage of Grace or a German one like the Peasants' War. In spite of long and complicated religious quarrels, actual martyrdoms were remarkably few, at least before the Covenanting troubles of the late Seventeenth Century. Organized and violent persecution on a great scale has been rare in Scotland: those who suffered most cruelly from it were witches. The phrase 'kindly Scots' has a double meaning. It emphasizes the Scottish sense of kinship, which carries with it a predisposition to kindliness in action, if not in words.

The face of modern Scotland is, of course, very different from that of earlier centuries. The low country and the coasts are still starred with small towns of stone, most of them completely rebuilt in the Nineteenth Century and surrounded, nowadays, with a rim of municipal houses in harled brick. Villages in the proper sense are a growth of the last two hundred years. The typical Scottish parish had its kirkton—church, manse, inn, and school—with farmhouses and clachans (*anglicé* hamlets) scattered over many square miles of country-side; and this is still the pattern in a good many remoter districts. But the population of such places has been growing thinner still. For more than a century and a half past, Scots people have been pouring into the cities, the growing towns, and the spreading agglomerations of industrial districts.

This process, now almost universal, began in Scotland earlier than in most European countries. Probably it has not gone quite so far as in England: an official estimate that 82.9 of the population is now urban is based on the very typically Scottish view that every community of 1,000 or more must be regarded as a town. But the greater part of Scotland has never been thickly peopled and though there is, perhaps, just a hint of recovery in the latest figures, much of it is emptier than it has been since census-taking began.

The country has, roughly, three-eighths of the area of Great Britain, but its people are only a little over five million, and this figure—about half the numbers of greater London—is increasing very slowly, if at all. In the century from 1801 to 1901 the population almost

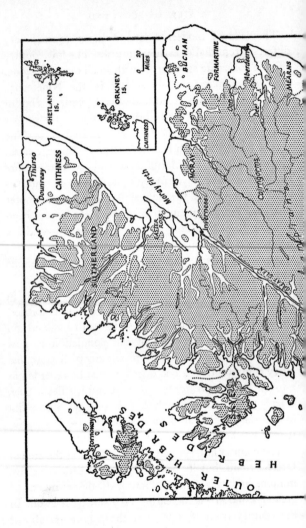

MAP OF SCOTLAND TO ILLUSTRATE REFERENCES IN THE TEXT

trebled itself—from 1,608,000 to 4,472,000. For the
first fifty years almost all parts of the country shared in
this expansion, though it was in the cities and industrial
areas that population soared. After this, numbers began
to shrink, first in the Highlands, then in the countrysides generally. In the last half-century the figure for
Scotland as a whole has risen by not much more than
14 per cent. (to an estimated 5,160,000 in 1957) and the
Highland population is less than it was in 1801. The
birth and death rates, which were 34 and 19 per
thousand in 1881, and 29 and 17 per thousand in 1901,
were 19 and 11·9 in 1956, so that, though the proportion
of older people has grown fairly quickly (more than
20 per cent. are now over 55 years old), the increase of
total numbers should have been well maintained.

The Scots, however, are an emigrating people. Even
before the New World opened to them, thousands of
young Scotsmen in each generation went abroad as
soldiers, traders, settlers—to France, Russia, and, after
King James VI became James I of England, across the
Border too. Though the Scots had their own colonial
schemes in the Seventeenth Century it is probable that
the first considerable group who settled beyond the
Atlantic were those who went as slaves, prisoners of war
shipped to the English colonies under Cromwell.
Highlanders cleared from their glens to make way for
sheep in the Eighteenth and Nineteenth Centuries sometimes travelled to Canada and the United States not much
more willingly. But most emigration has been voluntary,
and it has been on a scale unparalleled in the case of any
other West European country, except, perhaps, Ireland.

During the past 150 years men and women have poured into every part of the British Empire. Scotland supplied Canada with a large part of its population and many of its leading explorers, industrialists, politicians and bankers. Scots colonized the southern province of New Zealand. Many settled in Australia and South Africa. Hundreds of thousands have gone to the United States. There has been an almost constant migration to England. Over a million Scots-born people were living in the United States, England and Canada in the year 1931. Nearly half a million left the country between 1861 and 1901.

The process has accelerated since the expansion of population at home has been checked. Emigration in the fifty years 1901–51 amounted to 1,100,000 and in the one year 1957 it was reckoned at 32,510. The outward movement has been offset to some extent by immigration. At first this came chiefly from Ireland, but more recently the proportion of English to Irish immigrants has been reversed. In 1951 there were 231,794 people of English birth living in Scotland. But a loss of native Scots amounting to ·5 per cent. per annum is prodigious. For eighty years at least Scottish emigration has been heavier than English, not merely comparatively but in actual numbers.

These young people have been reared and educated in Scotland. It has been calculated that recent figures represent a yearly loss of more than £60,000,000 in capital outlay. And though some, no doubt, have gone in search of an easier way of life, or because, in one way or another, they could not reach the standards expected of them at home, many of them have been among the ablest and most ambitious of successive generations. The ancient habit of migration is never likely to be broken completely. Scotsmen like to believe that it is good for the rest of the world, and it has certain advantages for Scotland too. A population as concentrated as those of England and Belgium is scarcely to be wished for, and Scots abroad have undoubtedly helped to provide a market for Scottish exports. But when one considers that the outflow may actually exceed the natural increase, as it did between 1921 and 1931, and that Scotland's proportion of the total number of British people has fallen from nearly 16 per cent. in 1751 to 10.54 per cent. in 1951, it is difficult not to feel a certain anxiety about the future.

More than half the Scotsmen of today live in large towns. In some ways their environment is quite strikingly unlike that of English townsmen. The traditional character of most Scottish towns has been extreme concentration. The normal home was a flat in a tenement of three or four storeys, and most of these flats were very small: in Glasgow nearly half the houses are still of no more than two rooms, though the rooms themselves are apt to be rather large and high-ceilinged. This concentration has obvious disadvantages. In slum districts the overcrowding could be disastrous. But it has advantages too: undoubtedly it was the choice of the Scottish people who followed Continental fashions of building rather than English ones. When properly maintained, the tenement flat is warm and well-protected against the weather. Its tenants have the convenience or urban living close at hand—shops, schools, churches, public transport. The open country, too, is near. There are not many Scottish townsmen who need walk more than a few hundred yards from their doors to catch a glimpse of the hills. Half a century ago the outer tenements were apt to rise on the edge of ploughed fields dividing town from countryside as dramatically as the walls of a medieval city. Rising from the desk where these words are written I can be in the centre of Glasgow by train in ten minutes or by road can reach a hillside quite out of sight of any town in less than twenty.

During the past forty years rent control, combined with the Scottish system of rating which bore as heavily on the owners of houses as on their occupiers, has made the modernization, even the proper upkeep, of a great deal of tenement property almost impossible. Even stone walls have slowly deteriorated for lack of care. The building of Scots houses in the traditional style by private owners has almost ceased. When housing by local authorities began after 1918, the fashion was for cottages or two-storey terrace blocks with little gardens of their own. All Scottish towns are ringed with such buildings, but new tenements are now reappearing in the housing estates. Changes in the law of rents and rating look like making the repair and improvement of older tenements rather easier than it has been for more than a generation past. Slowly (too slowly), Scottish people have become rather more conscious of what was best in the national tradition of urban building. Now that the worst of slums are being cleared away and the sanitation of some Victorian buildings is being improved it seems possible that the cities will regain a good deal of the national character that they seemed to be losing, and that Glasgow, the largest of them, may learn to make more of the good looks of its handsome Victorian streets.

Glasgow is the centre of a 'conurbation' which, statistically, would seem to dominate Scotland even more decisively than London dominates England. A third of the Scottish people live in this area of Clydeside whose lines of building stretch, almost unbroken, for nearly thirty miles on end, from Dumbarton into central Lanarkshire. But in this case the statistical view can be a little deceptive. Psychologically and politically, Glasgow is not a capital. In the Middle Ages it was the ecclesiastical and educational centre of Western Scotland: since the Eighteenth Century it has been the centre of Scottish trade and industry, though not of banking. But though it has been the most populous Scottish city for a century and a half past, it has never made any serious effort to displace Edinburgh as the seat of the law, administration, and the General Assembly of the Church.

Perhaps to some generations of Glasgow men the boast that theirs was the second city of the British Empire seemed more satisfying than any claim to be recognized officially as the first city of Scotland. This boast is now only a memory. Glasgow itself, with just over a million inhabitants, has scarcely increased its population during the last half-century, though it has expanded physically to fill the valley between the

Kilpatrick Hills on the north and the Braes of Renfrewshire and Lanarkshire south of the Clyde. Plans for the rebuilding of its most crowded central districts involve the removal of perhaps a quarter of a million people to other towns. The conurbation round it is still growing, but in spirit (even in history) it is not simply an enlargement of Glasgow city. There are urban growths of the last seventy years or less which are true suburbs. But the older towns which are now linked physically with Glasgow are apt to have a formidable self-consciousness of their own.

One can catch some of the quality of this in Robin Jenkins' story about the years of depression, *The Thistle and the Grail*. Places like his Drumsagart do not feel themselves to be parts of Glasgow in any sense. And as the Clyde conurbation is not a solid social unit so its one and three-quarter millions are not the determining factor in the general life of Scotland.

There are smaller conurbations. Falkirk and its lesser neighbours stretch over fifteen or twenty square miles of East Stirlingshire: they are the centre of light castings and oil refining, and are growing. In Fife the mining and manufacturing area round Dunfermline is as large. But the capital of Scotland is unmistakably not a conurbation but a single, unitary city.

With less than half a million people Edinburgh is the second Scottish city in size. Since the Middle Ages, however, it has been the first in spirit and in architecture. It sprang from the rock which made a natural fortress long before the existing castle was reared there. Its backbone is the ridge of the Old Town, with its towering stone tenements reaching down from the Castle to the Palace of Holyroodhouse, on the edge of a wild park that contains the dramatic little mountain of Arthur's Seat. The Old Town was the Edinburgh of the kings and the parliaments. North of it, the New Town of wide streets and squares and splendid terraces belongs to the end of the Eighteenth Century and the early Nineteenth, to the first age when Scotsmen felt themselves rich. Between Old and New Towns is the green valley of Princes Street Gardens ending in a vast and still smoky railway station. And round the Old and New the city has spread out over a series of hills and ridges and down the northerly slope to the Firth of Forth, engulfing the once independent Port of Leith.

It is a city of wide views—towards the Highlands, towards the sea, towards the peaks of the Pentlands in the west, towards the last of the Border hills, south of them. It grows with some reluctance, and is apt to turn its back on the coalmines which are still developing on its outskirts. But it is the centre of government, finance and law, and as government becomes more pervasive new citizens are drawn into the capital, and new industries too. The great block of government offices, St. Andrew's House, 'the Scottish Whitehall', which was completed just before the last war is already too small for the Scottish Departments it was meant to house.

Scotland has two other large cities, Aberdeen and Dundee, each with a long history and each with about 180,000 people, more or less. Dundee stands at the mouth of the Firth of Tay on a magnificent site not too

skilfully used by its architects. It is a sort of eastern
Glasgow, as devoted to trade and industry (and, till
recently, as full of slums) though not so handsomely
built. Aberdeen is a provincial capital, the market and
university town of the North-East. Gleaming impressively, if a little coldly, in dressed granite, it looks
out over the North Sea, the northernmost centre of
important industry in Britain.

These four cities actually hold a larger share of the
Scottish population (38 per cent.) than similar great
towns have of England's. On the other hand, what are
officially called 'large burghs' (roughly, the towns of
over 20,000 people) have a smaller proportion. The
large burghs are scattered over the country from
Inverness in the north to Dumfries in the south-west.
Some of them are county towns, seven belong to the
Clydeside conurbation, nearly all are now industrial.
More typical, however, are the 'small burghs', with
populations from a few hundreds to 18,000 or so, where
the town life of the older Scotland often reproduces
itself more intensely. Some are almost wholly industrial,
but many are the capitals and markets of wide regions
and have a great place in historical memories: it is
notable that most of the medieval bishops' sees are now
small burghs (two are cities, three are not towns at all).
Such little burghs are apt to be the true centres of the
life of Lowland countrysides as they have been for many
centuries. Town life does not come naturally to the
Highlands. Most of the burghs there have been English-
speaking colonies among the Gaelic people: some of
them are so still.

This is a view of Scotland as the eye can see it and some glances at the past can help to explain it. It is a country as crowded in some parts as it can be, but, in the main, rather empty by European standards: highly cultivated where the soil allows, but often wild and sometimes very near desert, a country of long roads and wandering waters, with a people always more than half aware that they live on the edge of the European world. The rest of this book attempts to show what this people have made of it and of themselves.

Chapter Two

THE INDUSTRIAL SCENE

SCOTLAND is one of the oldest homes of machine industry: among industrial countries it may even seem old-fashioned, with its emphasis on ship-building and heavy machines, and the late development of mass-production plants. Its industry (indeed its trade on any very large scale) is scarcely older than the machine age, however. Perhaps it is true to say that before the Seventeenth Century the Scots as a people did not show any very intense interest in money-making, though they were organized for economic purposes in the usual medieval fashion. By any modern standard and in comparison with medieval England the country was poor, though not more so than a good many other parts of Europe. No doubt human greed was as common in Scotland as it is everywhere, but to the nation's active spirits liberty and religion meant more than wealth. A new impulse towards trade and manufacture came to most Western peoples as the wars of religion ended. For Scotland the change of mind was particularly dramatic.

In the first half of the Seventeenth Century Presbyterian Scotland made a prodigious effort first, under the National Covenant, to establish its own form of Protestantism against the pressure of its king, Charles I (who was also King of England), and then to impose this faith on its neighbours through its Solemn League and Covenant with the English Puritans. The fruit of the second Covenant was a frightful national disaster. The Scots, who had felt that they were fighting the Lord's battle and must be invincible, met the most crushing defeat in their history. For the first time the country was prostrate before a conqueror, Oliver Cromwell. It was occupied and annexed to the English Commonwealth. Even when, with the Restoration of Charles II, it regained its own parliament and government, it found itself almost ruined by the cost and the disappointment of the Covenanting Wars. The years of famine with which the century ended in Northern Europe filled the country with starving, angry beggars.

But in the moment of defeat, when their depression was deepest, the Scots had turned to plans for expanding trade and founding industries. They were almost without capital: even among landowners there was apt to be an acute shortage of actual coined money. Yet Glasgow, already the chief commercial city (though, for the only time in its recorded history, its population was actually shrinking) set about the business of providing itself with a port, its own river being too shallow for sea-going ships. There were projects for trading companies, for colonies, for factories—though this was long before there was powered machinery to operate them. Almost every important laird tried to create a market town on his own lands. Though their failure was less catastrophic, most of these plans were not much more successful than the great scheme for a Company of Scotland Trading to Africa and the Indies, with its colony on the Isthmus of Darien, into which

Scotsmen put a very large part of their available resources between 1695 and 1700. In the midst of national poverty there was much thought and discussion on economic subjects. William Paterson, who was largely responsible for the Darien Scheme, had been one of the founders of the Bank of England. His rival, John Law, was the creator of the Mississippi Company in France. In the last years of Scottish self-government, before the Union of 1707, Law brought forward a plan for providing the country with a paper currency based on its productive power—a very modern-seeming idea which was rejected by the Scots Parliament, largely because it seemed likely to bring 'all the estates of the Kingdom to depend on the government'.

The promise of free trade with the English colonies was the chief bait offered to Scotsmen in return for the Union with England which put an end to the Scottish State. Perhaps it was not quite so attractive a bait as has sometimes been imagined: in Glasgow, which had most to gain from dealings with America, opinion was so solidly against the Union that the police force of privileged burgesses was unable (evidently unwilling) to put down riots against it which lasted for more than a month. It was the Glasgow merchants, however, who took the first successful step towards the transformation of Scotland into a trading and industrial country. They won a great, finally a dominant, share of the jealously protected trade in colonial tobacco. Their ships brought the leaf from America to the Clyde. Nearly all of it was re-exported to the Continent or to England. For the first time a great stream of trading

profits gushed into Scotland. The ships which sailed
west for tobacco (and sugar) had to carry exports with
them. Markets opened for Scottish linen, the country's
chief manufacture, and for anything else that Scotland
could produce—boots, pottery, glass, iron goods. A
whole series of new industries came into being, some to
supply exports directly, others (like ropeworks and the
first chemical factories) to meet the needs of shipowners
or linen bleachers.

It is an irony that the theory of *laissez-faire* capitalism
and free trade should have flourished in a country
which owed its new wealth to the Navigation Acts—
the laws under which colonial produce could be
exported only to British ports and in British ships.
The Wealth of Nations was, no doubt, the most influential book ever published by a Scotsman, and Adam
Smith gathered much of his economic knowledge
during the years when he was a professor of Philosophy
at Glasgow and spent many evenings in discussion with
some of Glasgow's most intelligent merchants. But
there is a sense in which Adam Smith and his ideas
came naturally out of the Union. It is not surprising
that a people who had liquidated their own national
State should have been attracted by the thought that in
economic affairs (and a good many others) the State
ought to do as little as possible. During the century and
more when government direction of trade and industry
was dwindling, Scottish business did, in fact, flourish
most dramatically. Even in the tobacco trade Glasgow's
success was the result of free competition with English
ports which had been dealing with the American

colonies for a century: the Scottish merchants certainly received no particular encouragement from the British Government. Some government money already earmarked for Scotland was spent on the improvement of linen manufacture, but after this start Scottish industry relied on its own momentum. The commercial spirit which had survived generations of frustration was at last free to do its work.

The process shows up particularly clearly in Scottish banking. The Bank of Scotland, founded by an act of the Scots Parliament in 1695, was intended to have the same sort of exclusive privileges as the Bank of England. It was, however, distrusted by the British Government which encouraged the formation, in 1727, of a rival, the Royal Bank of Scotland. A third banking institution, the British Linen Company, grew out of the official plans for organizing and improving the linen trade. All these companies had, in a sense, political origins. All had their seats in Edinburgh. But all were, in principle, national bodies. They were not restricted by the English law which, in the interests of the Bank of England, made the development of a widespread branch system by other banks almost impossible. Their notes supplied Scotland with a currency that was badly needed. Their system of cash credits provided the founders of new businesses and progressive farmers with working capital. Many local banks appeared in Scottish towns, but by the beginning of the Nineteenth Century Scotland was developing a pattern of banking such as was scarcely known in England a hundred years later: a pattern of large joint stock companies each operating in several parts of the country, and all competing without exclusive privileges. Their £1 notes were used as freely as gold, and much more commonly. Scottish banking won a decisive vote of confidence in the crisis of 1797 when a quite illegal, though in practice unavoidable, suspension of cash payments was accepted by the customers. The country was, in fact, content to exist on its own credit, administered by its own bankers, and not backed by gold.

As a group these national banks, eventually including five with headquarters in Edinburgh, two (for a while four) in Glasgow, two in Aberdeen, and one in Inverness, were able to survive crises which brought about the collapse of many local banks in other countries. Even one or two failures among the leading Scottish banks themselves did not destroy a pattern which was widely copied, notably in Canada. The only privilege of the Scots banks was the right to notes of their own. This was secured to them permanently by the Act of 1845, which, however, cut at the basis of what had, in effect, been a free Scottish currency by limiting the fiduciary issue of each of them. Notes apart, English banks were perfectly free to enter Scotland, and some tried to do so. But the Scots banks were able to maintain what amounted to a joint monopoly of banking in Scotland. They even set up branches in London and (towards the end of the Nineteenth Century) in the north of England. There was no Scottish central bank, but two centuries after the Union the daily management of money in Scotland was almost wholly in the hands of Scotsmen.

The story of Scottish industry is not very different, though a good deal less smooth. When Adam Smith died in 1790, the new Scottish industrial economy had just found a way successfully through its first great crisis. The American Revolution had destroyed the principal colonial trade, in tobacco. Suddenly the basis of Glasgow's prosperity disappeared, but it very quickly found a new one. The technique of cotton-spinning by water-power had just been perfected in England. Linen had given Scotland many skilled weavers. Along Scottish rivers, particularly in the West, cotton mills sprang into being. The weavers of Paisley and Glasgow produced exceptionally fine cloths. Imports of cotton to the Clyde rose from 137,160 lb. in 1775 to 11,002,723 in 1811. Scotland was again able to export on a great scale, and again its trade was founded mainly on raw material from America.

To begin with, the second commercial age, like the first, depended very little on Scottish raw materials, except Scottish-grown flax. It used to be argued that our industries grew out of the accident which gave both Scotland and England coal and iron together. Coal was certainly important even a century and a half ago. It had been mined since the Middle Ages. Some of the first Scottish canals and railways were built to carry it. The first iron foundry to use Scottish coal and Scottish ores was established at Carron in 1759. Its most successful business was the casting of cannon, the famous carronades, but Scots iron was also used by the engineers who worked for the early cotton mills. Theirs was an auxiliary industry, however, like that of the chemists who supplied materials for bleachfields, printworks and dyeworks. James Watt had developed his steam engine with its separate condenser at Glasgow in 1765. He is notable as the most famous of a long series of Scottish mechanics who have had education as well as genius enough to make revolutionary changes in industrial techniques. But the coal-fired steam engine did not begin to affect Scotland very deeply until the cotton industry was well established. It brought the mills from the river sides into the towns. Mechanical weaving was added to mechanical spinning, but because Scottish cloths were particularly fine and, unlike Lancashire's, were made to be the cream of the international market, the skilled handloom weaver still held a place till the middle of the Nineteenth Century or later.

So far as Scotland is concerned the revolution of coal and steam may be said to have made its first great conquest at sea. The first commercially successful steamship in Europe was launched on the Clyde in 1812, ten years after what was perhaps the first practically useful steamer in the world had been seen on the Forth and Clyde Canal. Scotland was soon supplying the world with little steamers. Iron ships followed. The foundation of the great Clyde shipbuilding and engineering industries was properly laid. The railways, in their turn, were developed, for Scotland, by Scotsmen. By 1849 two companies had linked their services with London. But the Scottish lines remained independent. They stopped at the Border, or rather just beyond it. One English railway penetrated a few miles into Scotland. Again, as in the case of the banks, there had been nothing in law to prevent development in Scotland by English companies. The Scottish lines remained fiercely competitive with one another. By the end of the Nineteenth Century there were five of them, two managed from Glasgow, one from Edinburgh, one from Inverness and one from Aberdeen. The Scots could claim to have their own transport services as fully as the Dutch or the Swedes, though not quite so formally.

The chief Scottish industries were almost equally independent. Two native discoveries, that of the hot blast in smelting and that of the qualities of black band ironstone, in which coal was associated with ore, brought about an immense expansion of production after 1830. Scotland manufactured its own railway locomotives as well as marine engines. It exported both, as well as increasing quantities of other iron products and coal. At this stage the heavy industries began to displace textiles, and particularly cotton. As the American Revolution had killed the tobacco trade, the American Civil War, which cut off supplies of raw cotton, completed this new change. Only a few highly specialized cotton works and the great mills of Paisley, which became the centres of a world-wide empire of sewing cotton, survived the shock, though linen production continued on the East Coast and Dundee made itself the chief seat of jute spinning and weaving in Britain—for a time in Europe.

Steel followed iron. The chief foundries were near the Clyde. Their product went into ship plates, boilers, machines. Cast iron flourished near the Forth and in Glasgow. In the last years of the Nineteenth Century supplies of Scottish ore were becoming exhausted, but the skill of managements and workers and the equipment of the plants overcame this threat. The steel and iron industries continued to expand, using imported ores. Until electric power and the internal combustion engine began to change the face of industry and transport, Scotsmen were among the leaders of almost every sort of technical development. Some of these innovators and pioneers, like Watt himself; William Murdoch, who developed gas lighting and produced an early steam-automobile; Thomas Telford and John Macadam, roadbuilders; Kirkpatrick Macmillan, the inventor of the pedal cycle began as simple mechanics. Many others were the sons of professional people— Graham Bell, the inventor of the telephone, Lord Kelvin, who was great in telegraphy among many other things, and a long list of innovating technologists. For a century or more Scots people were able to feel that their country was at the very heart of the new industrial age. In fact the flow of practical ingenuity and technical imagination began to contract in the last Victorian decades, but this was scarcely noted for a time. Two hundred years after the Union, Scotland was one of the chief centres of metallurgical production in the industrial world. Coal was pouring from the mines of Lanarkshire, Ayrshire, Fife, and Lothian. The Clyde built more shipping than any other river.

The industrial Lowlands were certainly no paradise. Mills could be as satanic in Scotland as elsewhere. Brick-built mining villages were often squalid enough. The Glasgow slums remained a byword even when the foulest of them were cleared after 1866. There were years of depression and unemployment.

Adam Smith's gospel of greed was not, after all, a very pretty thing, though successive generations found it inspiring or reassuring. Some of its material results were hideous or cruel. Part of its spirit soon passed from masters to men. Politically, the Scottish working class were apt to be Radical. Their first leaders came from the weavers, a reading, arguing race. Trade unionism in Scotland was often the fruit of faith and intellectual conviction as much as a convenient means of protecting personal interests. There were many strikes, some fiercely fought, particularly in the mines. But by 1907, Scots labour leaders themselves looked hopefully to the future. They saw themselves advancing towards Socialism. They had their own Scottish Trades Union Congress, not opposed to the British one but to some extent independent and perhaps rather more radical. Though most of the Scottish Trade Unions have now fused with British ones, the S.T.U.C. survives.

In 1907 wages as well as profits and output in the mines and metal-using industries were high by the standards of the time. Other skills had also developed in the years that were past. The production of oil, distilled first from coal, then from shale, had called out new technical processes which were afterwards copied in America. Edinburgh had long been a seat of fine printing and paper-making. The world was acquiring a taste for Border tweeds and West of Scotland carpets were finding new markets for Scots wool.

And all, or almost all, of this had been created by

Scotsmen of the last few generations without the help or intervention of any political authority. Financially Scotland owed nothing to the British State. It seems fairly certain that, in the last years of the Nineteenth Century at least the Scottish contribution in taxes was above the British average. Under a system of free competition, the Scots could feel that they were doing a great deal more than paying their way in the world which, through their colonists, explorers, missionaries, soldiers, governors and merchants, they had been helping to open up around them. Except for two great American factories on Clydeside and one in Edinburgh, an important branch of Alfred Nobel's great dynamite international, and one great shipyard which had been taken over by an English steel firm, John Browns, most business in Scotland was wholly Scottish.

For the Scots economy, 1914 was the end of an age. The World War, which added some 140 service battalions to the Scottish regiments (and from which nearly 150,000 young Scots did not return) kept the heavy industries and farms in a feverish state of over-employment for four years. But the short post-war boom was followed in Scotland by two decades of almost unbroken economic depression.

Even before this slump had properly set in another economic change had appeared. The great increase in war-time taxation, which proved to be permanent, was draining free capital out of the country on a scale never imagined before. The official estimate of Scottish revenue rose from £19,950,000 in 1912–13 to £119,753,000 in 1920–1. British governments have never been willing to give figures which would show what proportion of Scottish taxes were, or are, actually spent in Scotland. No doubt the percentage was comparatively high in 1913, when the Government was spending freely on naval building. But there is not much doubt that (except perhaps in the worst years when Scottish unemployment brought a quite disproportionate flow of doles into the country) the loss of money has been high. It has continued: in 1952–3 the estimated revenue was £409,694,000, considerably more than the combined contemporary revenues of Norway and Denmark, and roughly equivalent to the revenue of Sweden or the Netherlands, both countries of much higher population and national income.[1] For Scotsmen accustomed to rely on their own resources, this situation was quite unexpected forty years ago. Industrial managements had been shaken by the war. It was an age of amalgamations. Four of the Scots banks were taken over by English ones. The Scottish railways were grouped under two great London companies. Locomotive building by the railways themselves ceased in Scotland and the independent Scottish industry had to find outlets abroad. Many individual firms, even in retail trade, lost their Scottish ownership. Many of the

[1] Annual White Papers giving estimates of the adjusted revenue and expenditure for (not in) England, Scotland, and Ireland ceased to be published regularly in 1922. Statistics for England and Wales, and Scotland were published in 1933, 1935 and 1954. Inflation accounts for part of the vast increase of these figures, particularly the last one. In spite of all, Scots seem to have continued to save rather more than their neighbours, but much of this invested money went, one way or another, to the British Government.

great Scottish shipping lines disappeared or transferred their headquarters to England. As the depression gathered there was a growing tendency to 'rationalization', which usually meant concentration of work nearer headquarters and markets in the South. One long-established industry, calico printing, closed down in Scotland altogether.

Shipbuilding and coal production had been at their peak in 1913. They fell steeply, and, in the early 1930s, when the slump became world-wide and cut down international trade on which Scottish heavy industries depended, the collapse became catastrophic. Shipbuilding fell (from 810,000 tons in 1913) to 74,000 tons in 1933, the lowest level since the triumph of steam, and 76 per cent. of the shipyard labour was unemployed. Between 1921 and 1931 the number of insured workers in Scotland did not increase, yet in the latter year 343,000 were idle, and this was roughly equal to the total figure of unemployment in Belgium, Denmark and Switzerland combined, at the moment of world-wide depression. Two years later the insured unemployed in Scotland reached 407,000 (more than 30 per cent.) and to this must be added at least 60,000 on poor relief. The streets of Scottish industrial towns were full of workless, hopeless men kept just above the level of starvation by weekly doles.

With the disorganization of world trade the whole atmosphere of industry had changed or was changing. Scottish industry had grown and flourished under *laissez-faire*. Now, almost for the first time since the Eighteenth Century, the British State was actively engaged in planning, supervising and protecting economic life. The disappearance of free trade gave little help to Scotland. The chief Scottish industries had been developed for a world market. The centre of the British market was in the South, near the seat of Government, and the new, highly protected industries gathered there. No doubt this was one reason for a failure to establish important automobile, aircraft, or radio factories in Scotland during the years of depression. For the first time Scotsmen learned what it could mean to live on the fringe of an economy which was at once centralized and contracting. There was some improvement as the world depression receded, but at the end of 1939, three months after the beginning of the Second World War, 10·6 per cent. of Scottish workers were still unemployed.

For the next eighteen years at least, unemployment in Scotland ceased to be a serious problem. Though it remained persistently higher than the English average and so tended to foster emigration, it was abnormal in no other sense. At the end of 1957 about 3·4 per cent. were without work. A pattern of revival seemed to have been working itself out: it was, perhaps, not so different from the pattern of 1913 as some people had expected it to be. Great efforts were made before the late war, and after it, to bring in light industries which might balance, even supplant, the established heavy ones. A large part of the industrial Lowlands became a 'distressed', then a 'special', finally a 'development' area which now includes the Highlands. Industrial estates were set up.

When a Scottish National Development Council was

organized in 1931, it soon found that one of its chief functions was to form a link between industry in Scotland and the expanding Government Departments concerned with economics in London. Yet even eleven years later, Mr. Thomas Johnston, perhaps the most effectively patriotic of all Scottish Secretaries of State, found that industry in Scotland was still tending to contract. The new factories for arms production had been concentrated in the South. Scots workers were being sent into England to help to man them. He set up a second body, the Council of Industry, to advise him in his efforts to check this process, which were notably successful. After the war these two institutions were fused into the Scottish Council (Development and Industry). Financed (rather narrowly) by business firms, local authorities, the Scottish Trades Union Congress and Scottish banks which are its members, the Council has helped to fill a gap, seldom felt in the days of *laissez-faire*, between the makers of economic policy and the Scots people.

It does, not quite officially, some of the work which would fall to a Department of Commerce in a self-governing State, besides much which no official body would be likely to attempt. It has certainly helped to bring in a good many new industries—the making of electronic and radio equipment, clocks and watches, business machinery, new chemicals and other work which should give employment to at least 150,000. Remarkably enough, more than 70 per cent. of the factories set up in Britain since the war by United States and Canadian firms have been placed in Scotland.

The Council has done its best to ensure that these, with factories established by English or Continental firms are, in fact, independent units with their own management and research staffs rather than branches which might easily be closed down in a slump. Possibly the Scottish Council's most important work has been to stimulate industrial research, which had been surprisingly weak in Scotland between the wars.

Though the Scots universities and technical colleges train an exceptional number of technologists, a high proportion of them find work outside the country, sometimes, perhaps, because they can learn more abroad than Scots schooling has been able to give them. In spite of the establishment in the new town of East Kilbride of a mechanical engineering research laboratory under the Department of Scientific and Industrial Research, Scotland's share in Government-financed work of this type is still pitifully small and the production (by private firms) of scientific instruments and machine tools is now much less important than it once was.

In the mid-Twentieth Century, as in the Eighteenth and Nineteenth, Scotland is learning new industrial skills. But the recent revival has still rested chiefly on the manufactures which Scotsmen built up for themselves in Victorian times and earlier: on shipbuilding, heavy engineering, steel-making. This has been a surprise to forward-looking planners, even to some industrialists themselves, who were inclined to expect, a few years ago, that the history of the early 1920s might repeat itself; that, in shipbuilding, for example, there might be a short boom while war losses were being replaced, followed by a long depression when it was found that the world had all the ships it needed. In fact, the demand for shipping grew for a decade, though it changed its nature with the increased output of oil tankers. The Clyde has not quite renewed its old supremacy or reached its old records: its output in 1957 was 417,177 tons. It was held up for a time partly by a shortage of steel: the pre-war contraction here seems now to have been overcome by the building of new plant. Scottish heavy engineering is finding a new outlet in the equipment of atomic stations. Three of these are built or building in Scotland itself—on the remote North Coast, the Atomic Energy Authority's great breeder-reactor plant at Dounreay, at the other end of the country the plutonium works of Chapelcross, Annan, and a power station at Hunterston, in Ayrshire, for the South of Scotland Electricity Board.

All this makes an encouraging picture, by the standards of twenty years ago quite astonishingly favourable. More can be added. For a time Scotch whisky was one of the chief dollar-earning exports of the United Kingdom. The Scottish Tourist Board, created by Mr. Tom Johnston, has done a great deal to bring strangers to a country whose people like to be visited. The North of Scotland Hydro-Electric Board, which also owes its existence to Mr. Johnston, its chairman, has been building dams, boring through mountains and supplying light and power to wide regions of the Highlands which had known nothing but oil lamps and candles, peat or sea-borne coal. It now controls all electricity supplies north of the Firths of Clyde and Tay, and since its foundation in 1943 has been substantially independent of the Central Electricity Authority. It relies for revenue largely on the sale of current to the South, but still draws heavily on loans for its constructive work. The South of Scotland Electricity Board, which covers the rest of the country, now has a similar independence. Besides its nuclear project it is building an enormous new power station at Kincardine-on-Forth. The Scottish Gas Board now manages all public supplies in the country. Through these three bodies Scotland has, in fact, regained most of the control which was lost when municipal electricity and gas and the private power and light companies were nationalized. It can, perhaps, be said that the tendency for ownership or management of Scottish industry to drift out of Scotland has been checked. More than half the new factories on the industrial estates are held by Scottish firms. The number of countrywide banking companies has again contracted but some are still owned in Scotland: one of the banks, the Royal, has reversed the more usual process of amalgamation by acquiring two important English subsidiaries. Banking is, no doubt, less of an energizing force than it once was. Some Edinburgh bankers are certainly not afraid of competitive innovations, and the Scots bank-note is still the currency preferred by most Scotsmen. Sentiment would be outraged if the familiar designs were to disappear. But the flow of notes and bank credit is now so closely controlled by the policy of British Governments that the share of financial independence they once gave to Scotland has almost gone.

In spite of their recent prosperity, Scotsmen are still apt to feel rather uncertain about their country's economic future. It seems vulnerable even to minor recessions. Nationalization of the coal-mines has been even less of a success in Scotland than in the South. Coal production has fallen from 41,300,000 tons in 1910 and 29,700,000 in 1940, to 21,330,900 in 1957. The cost of production is now well above the British average. Of 46 British mines marked down for closure in 1959, 30 are in Scotland. A large part of the Lanarkshire coalfield, on which other heavy industries relied for their growth is worked out. The National Coal Board has impressive plans for the sinking of new mines in the East of Scotland. Some have begun to operate, but the results, so far, have been disappointing. Hopes felt in 1945 that under nationalization substantial control of the Scots mines might remain in Scotland have not been fulfilled. The miners have been even more restive than they were in the last, depressed days of private ownership. Perhaps this is partly because, in coal-getting as in most other Scottish affairs, the natural unit is apt to be comparatively small and local knowledge and sympathy to be more important for management: partly, too, it may be due to the uncertainty of men who know that they may have to leave their homes for new ones in the developing coalfields.

While a new deep-water oil port has developed in the West, on Loch Long, sending its imports by pipe-line to a great new oil refinery at Grangemouth, which is attracting plastic and chemical factories, the native shale-oil industry is being strangled, not so much by any failure of its own as by a rigid Treasury policy which insists on taxing its products beyond its capacity. The nationalized railways, too, have been a disappointment. Though, for their purposes, Scotland is now a distinct 'region', as it was not under the inter-war grouping of lines, there have been few signs (at least until very recently) that the shape of the country with its concentration of heavy traffic in a narrow central belt and its large, thinly peopled areas, which, nevertheless, need to be served by some sort of transport (as they were served by the railways under Scottish ownership) demands a different kind of planning and treatment from what is most useful in English conditions.

Perhaps a Scottish Ministry of Transport might have been able to work out a better balance between railways, roads, shipping, and air service. Too little use is made, in these days, of the fact that most Highland communities have their feet in the sea. Bold and imaginative plans for the development of Scottish air transport and the industries that go with it on the pattern of Nineteenth-century shipping and shipbuilding, were foiled when two Government-owned airway corporations managed from London were set up: British European Airways, which hold a monopoly in Scotland, have frequently complained that their Scottish services are run at a loss. The Scottish Office now has responsibility for roads. There was real pleasure when the Secretary of State was able to announce that a road bridge would be built over the Firth of Forth, providing (at last) the most necessary link in any effective road system for the East Coast: but it will be a long time before Scotsmen forget the thirty years of argument and agitation which were needed before final approval for this parallel to the Forth Railway Bridge could be won from a British Government.

On the whole, then, the Scottish economy is moving. It is less self-directed, and consequently rather less self-confident than it was in the Nineteenth Century. It has lost a good deal of its financial independence, but it has recovered from the near-collapse of the 1920s and 1930s and has worked out, through the Scottish Council and otherwise, means of dealing with Government Departments and other authorities which are still too distant. Its national individuality remains unmistakable. Scottish industry is, in a sense, more marginal than it once was. If the country's experience of mass-production in the full sense, though growing, is still comparatively slight, we may be justified in remembering that managements and men in the chief Scottish industries are more practised in dealing with individually designed products, that automation is likely to replace most merely repetitive jobs, and that the future is likely to belong to the designers and skilled craftsmen.

It is one of Scotland's most serious weaknesses that, though its unskilled workers are comparatively well-educated and adaptable, as they always have been, it employs too few highly skilled specialists. This weakness could be overcome, since the facilities for technical training, especially through evening classes, exist and have been used for generations past. Scientific education seems to have lost a good deal of the liveliness that it once showed. Yet Scotland must depend almost entirely on knowledge, practical skill and equipment. It has very few native raw materials to work on—though, with proper investigation, the number of these could, no doubt, be increased. Even its supplies of coal are shrinking. It must be able to work up the products of other countries more effectively than their natives can do in an age when the knowledge of industrial techniques is spreading through the world. History shows, however, that precisely this sort of work was the foundation of large-scale industry in Scotland and that for two and a half centuries the country has drawn its main wealth from exports. It has been, and should still be, well-fitted to supply the sort of demand for capital goods which comes from undeveloped lands. While our present international trading system lasts the greatest need of Scottish industry will be that intelligence, training, enterprise, and direct contact with countries outside this island should not fail. For Scotland the freeing of trade with Europe is probably not something to be feared: its industries grew in such conditions and very nearly died when they ended. What is dangerous is remote control of Scottish business and the draining away of Scots intelligence and resources.

Chapter Three

LAND AND SEA

COMPARED with the towns and mainly industrial districts the land of Scotland stretches not wide but far. The arable acreage per head of population is almost twice that of England, and the proportion of rough pasture and moorland is, of course, enormously greater still. The number engaged in agriculture (105,200 in 1957) is certainly small by most European standards, but by British ones it is high, and farming's place in most Scottish minds is more conspicuous still because the fields are seldom out of even the townsman's sight for long.

Till the end of the Eighteenth Century the land made the background of life for the enormous majority of Scottish people. The old Scotland had not been a country of manors in the English sense but of farms, each shared by a number of tenants, not many of whom were secured in their holding by law or long-term lease, though where they had some sort of inherited link with the laird's family they could feel fairly certain that they were not likely to be disturbed. In the Middle Ages some monastic lands had been highly cultivated, but later they had suffered from war and the breaking up of abbey estates. The farm toun certainly formed a community. Its arable land was divided between infield and outfield. Only the first of these was regularly manured and ploughed. It was split into *riggs* or strips, separated not by fences but by *bauks* of unploughed earth, full of stones and weeds. Each tenant had his share of the riggs, on which he raised crops of oats, barley and peas. The outfield, too, was cropped as long as it would give a return in grain. It then lay fallow and was used for pasture till it had regained some fertility.

It seems likely that under this system the yield of most Scottish land had actually been declining for a century or two before the Eighteenth, while the population grew. Beyond the farm outfields the rough pasture was unimproved, and the country was gradually stripped of trees. For agriculture as for trade and industry, the air of the late Seventeenth Century was full of schemes of change. The last Scottish Parliaments passed a series of acts for the consolidation of holdings, the planting of woods and 'enclosure'—which, in Scotland, meant simply the building of boundary walls and fences. But very little was done. Till well into the Eighteenth Century the bare countryside was patched with little striped areas of ploughed land separated from one another by acres of rough grass, heather, and towering growths of broom. Here and there a castle or a laird's stone house stood out, perhaps with a few trees beside it and a large doocot, the pigeons from which plundered the tenants' corn and helped to supply the landlord's table. The farm touns were groups of low, heather-thatched buildings where tenants and cattle lived under one roof.

Perhaps the Union actually checked the movement

towards more productive farming, since it took some of the richer landowners to London. But the urge towards greater wealth soon began to assert itself among lairds. The Honourable the Society of Improvers in the Knowledge of Agriculture was formed in 1723. The joint tenancies were gradually (sometimes abruptly) ended. Land was given under long leases to improving farmers. New crops—turnips, potatoes, wheat, grasses— were introduced. Woods and windbreaks were planted. As new wealth flowed into the country lairds spent their money on drainage and building: their rents rose, and they were wealthier still. Scots inventors produced a new plough, then reaping and threshing machines. Stock-breeding was studied. Dairying flourished, particularly in the West. Land scarcely used before was tilled. By the beginning of the Nineteenth Century much Scots farming was as skilled as English and perhaps even more self-consciously 'scientific'. In some directions Scottish farmers were soon leading the agricultural world.

Villages grew, or, quite often, were carefully planned and laid out by the lairds. In Victorian times new churches and schools rose in them. They were villages of shopkeepers and artisans, however, for in Scotland farm workers lived (as many still live) in cottages or dormitory *bothies* belonging to the farms. Handsome country houses with highly cultivated walled gardens and tree-shaded 'policies' (*anglicé*, parks) replaced most of the old castles. New stone farm-houses, with their barns and byres, broke the rural view. The whole face of the arable countryside was changed. Marsh and heather retreated before new fields and pastures. Hills and moorlands which the plough could not conquer were starred with sheep.

There was, to be sure, another side to this process. 'Improvement' was enormously successful in the Lowlands. Though many of the old joint tenants lost their land there was often room for them on new farms or as labourers on the consolidated holdings: in any case, the expanding towns were close by. But in the Highlands, particularly in the West and North, the spirit of improvement miscarried. Chiefs and lairds who could boast of 30,000 acres or more were apt to feel that these wide lands should make them the equals in wealth of great lords and squires in England; but their lands were mostly moor and mountain. Current ideas of scientific farming did not work when they were applied to narrow patches of arable on the coasts and in glens already overcrowded with people who, as warriors, had once been more valuable to their chiefs than money but could not pay rent on the new Lowland scale. For a time the Highlands lived by rearing cattle. But it was found that sheep would pay better. They needed the glens for wintering as well as the hillsides, and they did not need men: a few shepherds (usually from the Lowlands to begin with) could take the place, economically, of whole townships of Highlanders—in origin the crofting township of the North was pretty much the Lowland farm toun.

The Highland Clearances swept scores of thousands out of their homes into the Lowland towns, across the Atlantic or on to narrow, almost untillable lands on the coasts (sometimes actually into huts built between the tidemarks, where the sea-wet earth was free to all), after 1770 or thereby. It was the potato, just come to the North when the Clearances began, which kept the North and West Highlands alive through years when population was still rising—that and fishing and the burning of sea-weed for kelp, which supplied industry with alkali during the Napoleonic Wars. With peace the demand for kelp fell away, and in the 1840s the failure of the potato crop, which brought famine and desolation to Ireland, struck a decisive blow at Highland life.

Before this, some lairds had made great efforts to accommodate the dispossessed, even when they themselves were on the point of bankruptcy. Others were more brutal. But even in the notorious Sutherland Clearances, when houses were burned to drive out the people, the landowner acted in the spirit of 'improvement', no doubt believing quite sincerely that his was the way of economic progress. It is characteristic enough that what is now the Royal Highland and Agricultural Society, founded in 1784 by optimistic Highland lairds, should have become (very usefully) the promoter of great annual shows, chiefly for Lowland farmers. In future these will be held only at Edinburgh.

In the West Highland and Isles, however, where each group of glens has its own qualities and difficulties, large plans and sweeping theories are no substitute for the most detailed local knowledge and understanding. Fifty years ago, when Scottish industry and Lowland farming felt themselves to be leading the world, the

Highlands were still a problem, as they are now. Even there, however, the atmosphere was more hopeful than it had been. This had become a land of great sporting estates—deer replacing the sheep which had replaced cattle on the hills—and of crofting peasants, living, more or less co-operatively, in coastal townships and eking out a living by fishing, spinning and weaving local wool, or occasional voyages as sailors. And they had just won security on their patches of land: after fierce struggles with lairds and the law, though tenants still, neither they nor their heirs could be displaced so long as the rent fixed by a Crofters' Commission, soon to become the Land Court, was paid. Land hunger was intense, but there was a belief that, through the breaking up of big estates, it could be satisfied.

In the Lowlands, as in other parts of Great Britain, farming suffered when free imports of food began to flow in from the United States and the colonial countries, but perhaps this late-Victorian depression was rather less severe than in England, largely because wheat had never been such an important crop—'corn' means oats in Scotland, as it means maize in America. Fewer new farm-steadings were built, but Scots farmers were quick to make use of each development in agricultural machinery, from the horse-drawn reaper-and-binder to the modern tractor. Even during the worst years of slump after 1918, Scottish Lowland farming was probably rather less badly hit than English. The family farm, particularly common in the West and North-East, stood up well to years of poor prices. Meat and milk production is Scotland's chief agricultural

business and Scots farmers grew more of their own
feeding stuffs. Skill was probably higher in Scotland,
and standards of life were simpler. In the 1920s and
1930s a good many farmers moved South and were able
to make a reasonable—sometimes a very profitable—
livelihood in districts where English farmers had failed.
But the depression was severe enough, and the first
efforts of the British Government to meet it, deficiency
payments for wheat and fixed prices for sugar-beet,
were of little value in Scotland where these crops were
not important, outside the Lothians, Fife and the
Laich of Moray. Organized marketing under statute of
milk and potatoes was more useful and was taken up
with some enthusiasm.

In the years of war and rationing, Scottish townsmen
became much more conscious of the farms. They
realized that (under war conditions at least) their
country was self-sufficient in meat, potatoes and milk—
that it was exporting a large part of its production. At a
pinch Scotland is, perhaps, almost capable of feeding its
own population, though habits of consumption would
have to change in such a crisis: there would be very few
of the wheat products which have such a large place in
the modern Scotsman's diet. It was natural that Scottish
farmers should do particularly well during the war.
Ley-farming and the growing of fodder were well-
established parts of their technique and helped to
increase milk production. In the post-war years farming
in Scotland, as in England, had a new prosperity.
Many farmers now own their land. Standards of living
have risen, though the number of landworkers still

shrinks. Seed potatoes go to many parts of the world, particularly, of course, to England. Scottish stock-breeding, Scottish beef and mutton have great prestige. Agricultural research, particularly at the Rowett Institute, Aberdeen, has built up a great reputation. Perhaps it can be said that Lowland farming is as well fitted to face competition as Scots industry has usually been.

The face of the Highlands has been more radically changed. There the years after 1918 were disastrous. Security of tenure had come too late to save the crofting system from decay. Though official policy had seemed to promise crofts to men returning from the war, land was found for very few of them. In the 1920s Canadian liners stood off the little island ports to take thousands of young people across the Atlantic. The land was left to the ageing and childless: country schools closed for lack of pupils, though the little Highland towns continued to grow. In the Outer Isles, where population was still very thick, thousands kept themselves going, rather ingeniously, on the dole.

The only constructive change was the planting or re-planting of forests, most of which had been stripped between 1914 and 1918. This was done chiefly by a new Government agency, the Forestry Commission. A large part of its work was carried out in Scotland, and particularly in the Highlands. Hillsides once lightly clothed in natural wood, birch, and scrub oak, were thickly covered with the blue-green of conifers. This gave some employment, but the new forests were only beginning to become productive when the second war came. Since then planting methods have been improved, largely with Scottish-made machinery: nearly half a million acres have been filled in Scotland, most of them in the Highlands. New villages for forestry workers have been built. Scotsmen now have a rather larger share in the control of Scottish forestry: this too is largely the work of Mr. Tom Johnston.

Mr. Johnston's Hydro-Electric Board (also a Government agency) has brightened Highland villages and flooded a certain number of glens. It is experimenting on a large scale with the use of Highland peat. Hundreds of thousands of acres of this fuel are still unexploited but it is doubtful whether the best means of using it have yet been found in Scotland. There are more hope and activity—and more children—in many districts, but in others the population has sunk so low that the social life and working co-operation in the crofting townships are almost destroyed. Revival is not helped by the educational policy which removes children over 12 from their homes for months at a time. Laws and rules made for an industrial population are apt to work out badly in the Highlands and Isles. It is ludicrous enough that, in the midst of a cattle-raising country, most communities of any size—even the moderately fertile island of Iona in its tourist season— should have to rely on imported milk. The Highland economy is, perhaps, distorted by a well-meant Government subsidy on hill cattle. Here and there this is actually producing new clearances.

This great region, which has few obvious natural resources except its extraordinary beauty, its water power, its forests, its seas and its narrow lands, can have very little economic future unless it makes the fullest possible use of its products at home. Deer forests and grouse moors no longer bring in much wealth. Beef cattle and sheep, though necessary to the economy, have to be sold out of the Highlands. Tourists are replacing the old shooting tenants. The Highlands and Isles have everything to offer them except an assurance of fine weather. But the Highlanders are failing to feed their visitors, or themselves, from their own land and seas as they could do. Over-regulation has something to do with that. A sort of apathy, the fruit of long discouragement, is as crippling: the people have found it too easy to accept doles of different kinds and imported goods and foods which are economically undesirable because they have to bear the cost of transport from distant cities.

Every generation for two centuries past has had its plan for solving 'the Highland Problem'. The results have not been encouraging; but today the combined efforts are, perhaps, more sustained and (on some levels) more intelligent. An official Highland Panel has been active in planning. A new Crofters' Commission has been set up to improve the use of Highland and Island land. It has the example of Orkney, whose small farmers (many of them not technically crofters only because they bought their land after 1918) have been extraordinarily prosperous for forty years past. The great naval base at Scapa Flow brought money into the rather depressed Orkney Islands during the First World War. This wealth was applied to the stocking and equipment of the windswept land. Orkney became one of the chief egg-producing counties in Scotland. It exported prize cattle and milk. It feeds itself remarkably well. The Orkneys are not the Hebrides, however. Their soil is deeper and naturally better drained. There is much less moor and hill land. The practical-minded, half Scandinavian Orkneyman is not a Gaelic Highlander. And even in the North Isles of Orkney the population, though prosperous enough, is falling.

The Crofters' Commission means to make sure that the land is worked—there are too many aged or absentee crofters—and to consolidate the smallest holdings where this is possible. It seems to have discovered that eagerness to turn crofts into small farms can be dangerous. In many places this might be the ruin of Gaelic social life, for there is not land enough for a community of farmers. There the crofter must have a second means of earning. In the Outer Isles the weaving of 'Harris' tweed—the wool for which is now spun chiefly in mills at Stornoway—provided a good many crofting households with a decent living: it does so still for some, though the partial closing of the American market to woollen goods brought some unemployment in 1957–8. The forests and some other small industries give part-time work. Mr. John M. Rollo has shown that it is possible to set up engineering workshops in the West (incidentally, his experience as a week-end crofter suggests that there are many untilled areas which could be profitably brought under the plough). Mr. Rollo is chairman of the Highland Fund, organized to provide capital for the kind of small-scale improvement and enterprise which is most needed in the crofting counties.

One would like to think it possible that these varying agencies may bring life back to regions which, a generation ago, seemed likely to turn into mere desert. The fact that the unemployment figures for the Western Isles have been higher than those for any other part of Scotland does not necessarily mean quite what it would elsewhere, but it prolongs and intensifies the inherited discouragement of the islanders. Such an episode as that of the British Government's plan for a rocket range in South Uist carries the sense of dereliction further still. This island was, on the whole, a prosperous one, with a sea-weed processing factory and weaving to balance crofting, and exceptionally lively Gaelic traditions when the rocket scheme was announced in 1956. It became clear that the life of the place was likely to be radically changed. Some of the best agricultural land would have to be surrendered. Many hundreds, perhaps thousands, of English-speaking Service-men would be stationed on the island and its neighbours. On the other hand, there would be paid work for all who wanted it. The old life of South Uist was considerably shaken. Then, with a change in defence policy, the plan suddenly shrank again. In 1959 the future of South Uist is quite uncertain and Highland and Island distrust of all official schemes is intensified.

Yet it can be argued that, in spite of all inquiries, advisory councils and committees, the possible resources of the Highlands—indeed of other parts of Scotland too—are still very imperfectly explored. The exploitation of dolomite in Skye suggests that there may be other minerals and useful materials to be discovered and that more might be made of the Highland shores and sea if modern technical knowledge could be imaginatively applied to them. Something is certainly needed to offset the decay of Highland fisheries.

Fishing has been an important thing in Scottish economic life. The seas round Scotland are rich. The crofter-fisherman was a part-time worker, but along the East Coast of Scotland are many towns and villages whose life depended on fishing. The city of Aberdeen, the centre of the industry, has been the third fishing port of Great Britain. The Firths of Forth and Clyde are also notable fishing areas.

Before 1914 the herring fishing was remarkably prosperous. The Scots output of cured herring (2,578,268 barrels in 1907) was the largest in the world. Most of this was for export, mainly to Russia, Germany, Scandinavia, and North America. Exports collapsed during the two wars. The Russian market was never properly recovered after the Revolution. The Soviet Union, Germany, and Scandinavia have developed their own fisheries. Trawlers (for white fish), drifters and smaller fishing boats were lost or decayed between 1914 and 1919. They were seldom replaced. Between the wars the Scottish fishing fleet was steadily ageing. There were few large fishing companies. Most boats were owned by individuals or families: their crews shared in the profits—or in the years of depression went penniless after losses. Successive Governments have refused to apply the Scots law, which should protect some of the fishing grounds from foreign trawlers.

The Fishery Board for Scotland which supervised this business in its days of expansion has been absorbed by the Scottish Home Department. In practice two new bodies, the Herring Industry Board set up in 1938, and the White Fish Authority (1951), do some of the work that it might have done. Both act for the United Kingdom, though the Herring Board's headquarters are in Edinburgh and the White Fish Authority has a strong Scottish committee. Schemes of regulation and contraction, of minimum prices and controlled sales sometimes seem to have distorted or restrained the trade, though they give a certain guarantee against the sort of shattering loss which fishermen often suffered in the early 1930s even when the catches were good. Recently there has been something like a competition in subsidies between the two Boards: that cannot be very healthy, but grants for new boats are allowing the Scots fleet to get rid of some of its ancient steam trawlers and drifters, and replace them with diesel-engined vessels. Scottish white fishing is, in fact, prosperous enough, and its landings have been increasing; but the herring fishery has not recaptured its old markets or found many new ones in spite of some ingenious planning by its Board. Exports stood at 63,500 barrels in 1956. In 1957 there were 10,400 Scottish fishermen: this compares with 32,000 in 1913.

Chapter Four

THE CHURCH IN SCOTLAND

IT was chiefly to safeguard the national Church of Scotland that the liquidation of the national State was accepted two centuries and a half ago. This gives the Church a peculiar place in Scottish history. Today its place in the life of Scotland is almost equally unusual. The record of God's works through the Scots would make a story scarcely less dramatic than the *Gesta Dei per Francos* and in this century's eyes perhaps more admirable: beginning with the first great missionary journeys from Iona it would show the building up in Scotland of one of the most influential and widespread forms of Protestantism, then a crusade (luckily shorter than the Franks'), then a second great wave of missionary work and the successful assertion, in this part of Britain, of the absolute independence of a national church in a supra-national state.

Even from a wholly secular point of view, the church in Scotland is notably important. The tradition of the Scot who sups theology with his porridge is not much more than a memory nowadays, though it is true that Scotsmen are very ready to argue on such questions, as on other things: it is difficult to think of another country where long letters quoting Pope Gelasius I and Theodoret would interest the readers of a daily newspaper as they certainly interested Edinburgh people in 1957. Reports of church courts that have denounced dancing or the Duke of Edinburgh's Sunday polo occasionally startle or amuse the rest of the world, which does not realize that the Free Church of Scotland, or the Free Presbyterian Church, the sources of such pronouncements, are tiny sects scarcely known outside the Highlands. The majority of adult Scots today, however, are active members of some church, and the Church of Scotland itself, still recognized by the State, and at the same time completely free from any sort of State control, has, in the past, done more to shape the character of Scottish life, of Scottish political and social habits, than any other national institution.

There is a sharp contrast here between Scotland and other English-speaking countries. In the United States, the white Dominions, and Wales, the Protestant majority are divided between a number of sects not very unequal in importance. In the Irish Republic the Roman Catholic Church is the national one. In modern England the National Church, partly controlled by the State, has rather more members than the dissenting Free Churches, but perhaps rather fewer than are claimed by the Roman Catholic Church. Perhaps three adult English people out of four, however, seem to have no active place in any religious body. The Church of Scotland, on the other hand, is enormously stronger than any other in the country. Its communicant membership (officially 1,307,573 in 1956) includes more than a third of all adult Scots—nearly half of them, if 'adherents' (who have not joined the Church but attend its services) are included. Next in numbers are the Roman Catholics with about half a million adults. The Episcopal Church in Scotland (Anglican) claims 56,000. Four small bodies, which share the Church of Scotland's traditions—the Reformed Presbyterians, the Free Church of Scotland, the Free Presbyterian Church and the United Free Church—have some 40,000 between them. About 140,000 belong to other Protestant sects — Methodists, Congregationalists, Baptists, 'Brethren'.

The Church of Scotland is Presbyterian. It may be said, indeed, to have formed the pattern of Presbyterianism as this is known in other English-speaking countries. Its organization is a hierarchy of courts or councils. Each congregation has its kirk session, consisting of elders, laymen elected (or accepted) by the members, with the minister as moderator (president). Each kirk session is represented by the minister and one elder in the presbytery which exercises some of the powers that belong to bishops in episcopal churches. There are sixty-six Scottish presbyteries, very unequal in size. More than 250 kirk sessions are within the bounds of the Presbytery of Glasgow, seven in the Presbytery of Islay. The presbyteries are grouped in twelve synods, meeting twice a year.

The parliament of the Church is the General Assembly which meets annually in May. Once in four years every Scottish kirk session sends its minister and an elder to the Assembly in Edinburgh. The Assembly is a legislature. It passes acts for the government of the Church, receives and debates reports of commissions and committees, and makes 'deliverances' on them.

It is also a law court which decides cases of discipline and disputes, generally on appeal from the lower courts. A High Commissioner represents the Sovereign at each Assembly, but though he addresses the members the gallery from which he speaks is not technically a part of the Assembly Hall, and he himself is not the president: indeed, he is not a member, unless he has been sent there as an elder. The Assembly formally elects its own Moderator, who has been nominated by a special committee. He holds office for one year only, and though he is, in practice, the chief representative figure of the Church, and its spokesman, he has no powers except those of a chairman. Indeed no single minister has permanent authority over any other. The Assembly itself is not fully sovereign, in the sense that the British Parliament is sovereign. Any proposal which would make a serious change in church law or practice must be submitted to the presbyteries after the Assembly has 'received' it. It can become a permanent Act only if two-thirds of the presbyteries accept it.

This form of organization, rather than anything in its theological standards, gives the Church of Scotland its peculiar character and has allowed it to make its most decisive mark on Scottish life. The system is sometimes called 'democratic', but this must be a misleading description for any organization which seeks to express the will of God rather than the wills of men. The Kirk's constitution was worked out long before political democracy in the modern representative sense had been developed. It is, however, by far the completest expression of the Scottish attitude to the business of government: more effectively than anything else in Scotland's past or present—far more effectively than the old Scottish Parliament—it combines the national will for a form of administration which will work with the national distrust for absolute human authority. No doubt this is one reason why, in 1707, the Scots were ready to sacrifice their parliamentary independence on condition, and only on condition, that the independence of the Kirk was preserved by an Act of Security which was fundamental to the Treaty of Union and which every British sovereign must swear to uphold.

The system was complete before the end of the Seventeenth Century. It has scarcely changed since. Authority remains in the Church of Scotland—in other Presbyterian churches too—but it is carefully diffused. The authority of the minister is safeguarded by the laws of the Kirk: ministers take the lead in church courts, where they are moderators. But 'ruling elders' and, in a sense, the congregations they represent, share authority too. From one point of view the minister is a bishop, the lay elders his presbyters. From another the presbytery is a sort of bishop-in-commission. But there is no Presbyterian papacy, not even a joint one. The Church of Scotland must try to reach its ends by agreement—the agreement of the majority of a kirk session, of the majority of presbyteries (and, finally, of the congregations behind them) in any great national decision. Throughout its history this is what it has usually succeeded in doing: its occasional failures have produced the great crises of its past.

The system itself has grown out of history. Christianity in Scotland goes back to the time when the little kingdoms were forming in the last days of the Roman Empire. Its missionaries were natives of the country or Irish monks who carried the Faith from St. Columba's island settlement in Iona to the North of England. As in most Celtic countries, the organization of their church was mainly monastic. In the first feudal age the Church in Scotland was fitted into the normal medieval pattern, largely by a royal saint, the Anglo-Saxon Margaret, and her sons and great grandsons. The country was divided into bishoprics; monasteries of the Latin tradition were founded, Benedictine, Cluniac, Tironensian, Cistercian, Premonstratensian, Valliscaŭlian; secular priests were settled in parishes; the friars were received.

This *Ecclesia Scoticana* was directly dependent on the Papacy. During the struggle for national independence its clergy were notable patriots, and, later, the Stewart kings leant on the loyal support of its hierarchy. But the endowments of many of its parishes were diverted into monastic hands. Its churches came to be served, too often, by ill-instructed priests who were forced to wring a poor living out of parishioners even poorer than themselves. The rich bishoprics and abbeys were used to endow the sons of great families. At the beginning of the Sixteenth Century the revenues of the Archbishopric of St. Andrews, the primatial see, were held by two royal boys successively. Neither was ever consecrated, and each held a great abbey as well as the archbishopric. At the moment of the Reformation five royal bastards held six great religious houses among them. One of them, James Stewart, Prior of

St. Andrews, became the ablest leader of the Protestant nobles.

The fall of this system came, in appearance, very suddenly, and, in the chronology of the Reformation, very late. The Parliament which, in 1560, broke with the Papacy, approved a Protestant confession of faith and forbade the saying of Mass, was in many ways an irregular body, held without the sovereign, Mary Queen of Scots (who was also Queen Consort of France). The monasteries were not formally dissolved. There were no public martyrdoms of Roman Catholics in the Sixteenth Century, in spite of the Act which threatened death to those who persistently celebrated or heard the Mass. Most Church revenues remained in the hands of those who held them, often laymen. Within a year of the revolution Queen Mary, now a widow and no longer Queen of France, was in her own country. She was a sincere Roman Catholic and the natural rallying point for a Counter-Reformation.

Yet the rulers of the old Church scarcely raised their heads again. There were, indeed, prolonged civil wars between groups of nobles who stood, more or less, for one religious system or the other. At first the courageous and unlucky Queen was concerned in some of these, but in defence of her crown (or herself) rather than of her religion. The leading Protestant party usually had the support of her enemy, Queen Elizabeth of England. In the course of these troubles the Archbishop of St. Andrews was captured in armour and hanged as a rebel: he was, indeed, no more than one of the leaders of a family feud. The new ideas of the Reformation had, in effect, conquered the Lowland towns before the Roman Church fell. They were supported, in Scotland, as in so many European countries, by powerful laymen who had their hands on the Church's wealth, and in the following centuries they were never seriously shaken.

The Reformation was not, however, an act of State in Scotland as it was in nearly all other lands where it was successful. In England, Scandinavia and the German principalities, the rulers themselves declared for reform, and usually succeeded in absorbing much of the fallen Church's riches and power. In Scotland, the great change was made in defiance of the Crown.

When the baby, James VI, was set up as King after his mother's defeat, the Protestant Government which used his name was a revolutionary one. Very little of the old Church's wealth ever came effectively into his hands: not much more reached the new Kirk of Scotland. But the spiritual power, the independent authority of the Church did not pass to the State. Protestantism could scarcely have established or maintained itself under Scottish conditions without an unshakeable conviction both among its leaders and among great numbers of laymen, that religious truth was more important than any human consideration whatever.

From its beginnings the new Church was a preaching one; it relied on the power of the Word. Because it was exceedingly poor and could seldom trust for very long in the backing of any government it needed the organized and active support of the people. Readers of John Knox's *History of the Reformation*, the extraordinarily vivid apologia of the Kirk's first great leader, are apt to be shocked by the vigour with which he dramatizes his own debate with his Queen and glories in having brought this charming and intelligent but almost defenceless girl to tears. To understand Knox one has to realize that he felt himself to be a prophet, defying all the constituted authority of this world in the name of the Lord. The shape of the Church of Scotland and of Scottish history in the last four centuries has come out of this conflict.

'There are two kings and two kingdoms in Scotland', said Knox's successor, Andrew Melville, to Queen Mary's son. 'There is Christ Jesus the King and His kingdom the Kirk, whose subject King James the Sixth is, and of whose Kingdom not a king, nor a lord, nor a head, but a member.'

Melville was the true organizer of Scottish Presbyterianism. Knox, who had lived in Calvin's Geneva as well as in Protestant Germany and England, was a Calvinist in theology. Though his party leant on England politically, he had laid the foundations of a Reformed ecclesiastical system in Scotland itself on a consistorial Continental pattern rather than an English one. He had, however, introduced or accepted superintendents of districts who had some of the powers of bishops. This was avowedly a temporary arrangement, meant to meet an emergency in which there were far too few educated ministers to fill the vacant pulpits. It might conceivably have grown into a sort of episcopacy, however, if the politicians of the time had not tried to introduce titular bishops who had no real functions except to convey the wealth of the bishoprics to their noble patrons—and if Andrew Melville had not appeared with his passion for the independence and perfection of the Kirk.

Melville was a man of immense energy, universal learning, and vivid intelligence. It was he who developed the presbytery as a court supervising individual churches. Once it was established, there was no place in the Kirk for superintendents or bishops, and though James VI eventually re-established episcopacy and sent Melville himself into exile, the King's bishops remained, in the eyes of most Scots Protestants, a sort of royal police force set up to limit the Church's freedom, always suspect and, from the point of view of working organization, strictly unnecessary.

What was necessary was an educated (or at least literate) laity, able to read the Bible, from whom elders might be drawn, fit to work with the ministers trained in the reformed Universities. This need set the pattern for Scottish education. The system of diffused authority was extraordinarily resilient. It ruled the nation during the Wars of the Covenants, when Scotsmen fought against Charles I to secure 'the Crown Rights of Christ', first in Scotland itself, then throughout the British Kingdoms. But even in defeat and failure, when Cromwell had dispersed the General Assembly as well as the Scottish Government, and during the years when the last Stewart kings were trying to impose on Scotland bishops more or less of the Anglican kind, the eldership, the kirk sessions and the presbyteries still persisted. In 1690, when James VII and II had been driven overseas, the Presbyterian Kirk of Scotland emerged again,

national and largely independent of the State, though
no longer bent on forcing Presbyterianism on the neigh-
bour nations.

Two minorities refused to enter this revised national
Kirk. Today they are represented by the Episcopal
Church in Scotland (now closely linked with the Church
of England) and the Reformed Presbyterians, the heirs
of those enthusiasts who believed that the Presbyterian
manifesto called the National Covenant and the treaty
with the English Puritans called the Solemn League
and Covenant were, in fact, contracts between God and
the Scottish nation which must never be abandoned.

At this point the resilience of Presbyterianism began
to show itself in a new form, and one that, for nearly
two centuries, seemed to threaten the Kirk's existence.
If the Presbyterian polity could not be crushed it could
split. When dissenters broke away from the Church of
England or many of the Continental churches they
could seldom carry their bishops with them. New sects
had to find new forms of organization for themselves.
But in Scotland any dissenting minister and his congregation could form a kirk session of their own. Any
group of rebel ministers could declare themselves a
presbytery.

In many Presbyterian minds the parliamentary Union
with England had roused deep doubts and suspicions,
though it had been accepted largely because it promised
to safeguard the Kirk against the danger that Roman
Catholic Stewarts might come back to the Scottish
throne. Could it ever be right or safe that the Presbyterian Scotland should be ruled by a prelatic parliament

in London and by foreign kings who would not adhere to the Scots Covenants? Those doubts were confirmed when the British Parliament broke the bargain made at the Union, destroying by a new law the right of the representatives of parishes to elect their own ministers. Throughout the Eighteenth Century and nearly half the Nineteenth this restoration of patronage (the nomination of ministers usually by local landowners) produced a series of convulsions in the Kirk. And there was soon dissent among the dissenters themselves. The first Secession divided itself into Burghers and Anti-Burghers, New Lichts and Auld Lichts, Lifters and Anti-Lifters.[1] The Relief Church which followed it into dissent was less fissiparous. Finally, in 1843, when, with a revival of evangelical feeling, the sense of the national Church's right to the completest spiritual freedom had also revived, there came the great Disruption. Four hundred ministers left their parishes (and their homes and stipends) to form, with at least a quarter of a million lay people, the Church of Scotland Free, because British politicians refused to allow the Kirk to rid itself of the effects of patronage.

'The most honourable fact for Scotland that its whole history supplies', wrote a wise and engaging memoirist, Lord Cockburn, who did not leave the Established Church himself. Certainly it was a remarkable

---

[1] Anti-Burghers rejected an oath required from burgesses of Scottish towns because it seemed to imply recognition of the Established Church. Auld Lichts (Old Lights) insisted that the civil power should have a duty to impose (Seceding) orthodoxy on all. Anti-Lifters forbade ministers to raise the communion elements during the consecration service.

thing in an age and country generally supposed to have been peculiarly absorbed in the business of money-making. With no resources except its members' gifts, the Free Church raised buildings and settled its ministers in nearly every Scottish parish, set up colleges and schools, took over the whole missionary work of the Church of Scotland—for every missionary had seceded. It had, of course, its own Assembly, synods, presbyteries. Indeed it duplicated the work of the Established Church. As Scotland's population was growing very fast, this duplication met real needs of the time. But though the Disruption released remarkable energies it also established a view of Scottish Presbyterianism (and Scottish society in general) which will be found in most histories written half a century or more ago, and still has echoes.

Scotsmen, and the Scots Churches in particular, it was argued, are incapable of holding together. In fact, new schisms did appear after the Disruption: of the four dissenting Presbyterian churches that still exist only one is older than 1843. But already before the Disruption the resilient adaptability of the Presbyterian system had begun to work in the opposite direction. If it is easy for Presbyterians to divide when they differ, it is almost as easy for them to reunite when the grounds of difference disappear. Presbyteries and assemblies can merge again. In 1820 the oldest bodies of seceders began to come together. In 1847 most of them joined in the United Presbyterian Church. In 1900 the great majority of the Free Church (heirs of the Disruption) and the United Presbyterians formed the United Free Church of Scotland. In 1929 almost all congregations of the United Free Church merged again in a national Kirk which had liberated itself completely from any claim of King or Parliament to control it in spiritual matters. Patronage had been abolished by statute in 1874: henceforth congregations chose their own ministers. As a prelude to reunion Articles Declaratory of the Church of Scotland's constitution had been passed by the General Assembly in 1919 and recognized by Act of Parliament in 1921.

'This Church', the Articles assert, 'as part of the Universal Church wherein the Lord Jesus Christ has appointed a government in the hands of Church office-bearers, receives from Him, its Divine King and head, and from Him alone, the right and power, subject to no civil authority, to legislate and to adjudicate finally, in all matters of doctrine, worship, government and discipline in the Church. . . . Recognition by civil authorities of the separate and independent government and jurisdiction of this Church in matters spiritual, in whatever manner such recognition be expressed, does not in any way affect the character of this government and jurisdiction as derived from the Divine Head of the Church alone, or give to the civil authority any right of interference. . . .

'This Church acknowledges the divine appointment and authority of the civil magistrate within his own sphere. . . . The Church and the State owe mutual duties to each other, and acting within their respective spheres may signally promote each other's welfare.'

No statement of the doctrine of the Two Kingdoms could be firmer or more comprehensive than this one, and none could have been more unreservedly accepted by the State. This is a remarkable triumph for the principles of Andrew Melville. Indeed it is difficult to understand how it has been possible since 1921 to maintain the well-known theory of English constitutional lawyers that the British Parliament is absolutely sovereign in all things.

Thus the Scottish ecclesiastical history of the past century is one of reunion. Now, as in 1690, the great majority of active Scottish Protestants form one body, though at each union a small minority of one of the sects concerned maintained its independence. But though, when compared with some other national churches, the Kirk is remarkably strong, its circumstances are obviously very different today from what they were at the end of the Seventeenth Century. The annual meeting of the General Assembly still gets something of the same sort of public attention that is given elsewhere to the opening of a parliament. The Lord High Commissioner, holding court at Holyroodhouse, is a viceroy, for ten days in the year. In some ways the Kirk is more self-sufficient than it ever was: in their years of separation from it the dissenting bodies which have now returned learned to pay for their own buildings, ministers, and organization through their members' gifts rather than from endowments or tiends (tithes). This experience has made it comparatively easy for the Church of Scotland to finance itself without reliance on the State. Most of its inherited property is now held for it by General Trustees, but by far the greatest part of its funds comes from its members. It maintains missions in India and Pakistan, in South, West, and East Africa, in Arabia, Hong Kong, and Jamaica. It has built scores of churches in new housing areas under its National Church Extension Scheme. Its 'social services' are expanding—homes for old people and children who need care, hostels for youths and girls. A peculiarly individual agency, the Iona Community, whose leader, the Very Rev. George F. Macleod, was Moderator of the General Assembly in 1957, combines social work and evangelism in the cities with study and re-building of the medieval Abbey on the Isle of Iona. It attempts to emphasize the collective nature of the Church's work and has a considerable influence on younger ministers.

On the other hand, the Kirk no longer controls Scottish education. It ceased, more than a century ago, to be the recognized guardian of the poor. The local church is seldom the centre of the life of its parish: indeed, partly as the result of dissensions and reunions, the parochial system itself has broken down, especially in the towns. Congregations are scattered and inter-mixed in a way that complicates, though it scarcely cripples, the work of the eldership.

It is often said that the Kirk has lost touch with the industrial workers. Perhaps this is actually rather less true in Scotland than in some other countries. Industrialism has raised barriers against religion in most parts of the world. It is doubtful if there is a Scottish 'church-less million'. But the days when Scotland lived, intellectually, on the Bible and the Shorter Catechism have certainly gone.

With the decay of orthodox Calvinism, religious knowledge has weakened even among regular church-goers. New enterprises of evangelism, notably the Tell Scotland movement, are, in part, a reaction to this state of things. Their effect has been considerable notably among younger people, but their emphasis has not always been intellectual.

Under a system of councils and committees whose members are usually anxious to avoid open disagreement, kindly compromises on disputed questions are, perhaps, too easily found. The Kirk is certainly not a bigoted and exclusive body. Its communion services are open to all Christians. In its eagerness to show that it is free from narrowly national prejudices it is sometimes oddly neglectful of its own traditions. For a century past its services, even its buildings, have shown an anglicizing tendency. In his important book on *The Architecture of Scottish Post-Reformation Churches*, Mr. George Hay writes of 'well-meaning clerics [of the recent past] to whom "the beauty of holiness" meant a gothic Anglican church planned according to Victorian precepts . . . as though the Kirk had finally turned its back on Geneva and its Reformed and Continental affiliations'. Yet in spite of unnecessary chancels and altar-like communion tables, even dedications to St. George or St. Bride, and the discreet use by ministers of a Book of Common Order, there are very few Church of Scotland services which could be mistaken for those of a more hierarchical sect, and the reactions to a proposal made in 1957 that, in the interests of 'closer unity' with Anglican bodies the Kirk should consider the acceptance of a form of episcopacy does not suggest that the majority of Scottish Protestants are at all likely to abandon their national Presbyterianism.

The Church of Scotland now has a rival which can scarcely be said to have existed in the country two and a half centuries ago outside a few islands and a handful of inland pockets, mainly in the North-East—a rival far more formidable than any Protestant sect. It was industrialism which brought back the Roman Catholic Church to the Lowland cities. Irish immigrants and a certain number of Highlanders and Islesmen filled the first town chapels built between 1808 and 1850. The hierarchy was re-established in 1878. There are now two archbishops and six bishops, and the Roman Catholic population is not far short of 700,000. This includes perhaps rather less than half a million adults practising their faith, who may reasonably be compared with the members of Protestant churches.

Very naturally, this restored Church has done what it could to emphasize its right to represent the medieval *Ecclesia Scoticana*. A high proportion of its prelates have been chosen from the districts, small as these are, which remained Roman Catholic after the Reformation. But the great majority of its people are still the descendents of immigrants—Irish, Italian, Lithuanian, Polish —and its chief strength is in the industrial West.

It can be said that their Church has done nothing to check the growth of national feeling among these new Scots. Religious prejudices which were apt to become violent in the years of heavy immigration when Ireland sent over Ulster Protestants as well as scores of thousands from what is now the Republic, have tended to dwindle as the number of incomers has fallen, but in public affairs the Roman Catholic Church is, by its nature, an isolated body, and perhaps it is true that its place in the national life is still smaller than statistics might suggest.

Chapter Five

SCOTLAND AT SCHOOL

SCOTLAND has long been a country of former pupils. Characteristically enough, Scots people seldom speak of themselves as 'old boys' or 'old girls' of a school: they prefer the more official-sounding phrase. Old-boy-ishness, indeed, is not a very typically Scottish state of mind. Comparatively few make pious pilgrimages to the classrooms where they sat twenty years ago. But practically all Scotsmen and Scotswomen have many generations of schooling behind them. In principle at least, universal education is now a commonplace throughout the civilized world, but for most peoples this is a fairly recent experience, as history goes. It is not so for the Scots. Compulsory education, to be sure, goes back less than a century, but general education, the habit of schooling for people of every class, is something that stretches into the past far beyond living memory.

This habit has certainly helped to form the modern Scottish people. Unlike the Church and the law, the national system of education was not specially protected by the Union of 1707, though the Treaty professed to safeguard the rights of the Scottish universities. In effect, however, the schools were fairly secure because they were very much the Church's affair. The system was already national. It had been formally established by an Act of the Scottish Parliament ten years before the Union. But, in practice, it scarcely depended on the State. This fact tended to develop some of the special characteristics of Scottish education.

No doubt Scotland was fairly well provided with schools before the Reformation, considering its comparative poverty. In the Fifteenth Century it supplied itself with three universities: at St. Andrews (1411) and Glasgow (1451) which were soon to be the sees of archbishops, and at Aberdeen (1494), the chief city of the North. But it is a document of the Reformation, the first *Buke of Discipline* (1560), which gave Scotland the framework of an educational system. John Knox's plan for the schools and universities remained no more than a programme in his day; for the Reforming politicians, though they approved it, were unwilling to pay for it out of the spoils of the Roman Church. But it is a programme which guided the development of Scottish education over three and a half centuries and supplied the ideas about schooling which still come most naturally to Scottish minds.

'Seeing that God hath determined that his Church here on earth shall be taught not by angels but by men', care must be taken that all children are given learning enough to understand their religion. There must be a school at every church: if there is a village the schoolmaster should be able to teach grammar and Latin. In every 'notable town' there should be a college, teaching Latin and Greek, logic and rhetoric—in fact, a secondary school. The poor, especially boys from the country, must be helped to attend such schools. All those who are fit to study at a university must be encouraged to go there.

'The rich and potent' are to be compelled by the Church to educate their children at their own expense. 'The children of the poor must be supported and sustained on the charge of the Church till trial be taken whether the spirit of docility be found in them or not. If they be found apt to letters and learning then may they not (we mean, neither the sons of the rich, nor yet the sons of the poor) be permitted to reject learning; but must be charged to continue their study, so that the Commonwealth may have some comfort by them'. Two years would be enough, Knox thought, to learn reading, the catechism and the beginnings of grammar—that is, for an elementary education. Secondary education might take seven, 'which time being expired, we mean in every course, the children must either proceed to further knowledge or be sent to some handicraft or to some other profitable exercise; provided always that first they have the form of knowledge of the Christian religion'.

For the Sixteenth Century this was a prodigious plan. It was scarcely realized at the end of the Nineteenth: so far as knowledge of religion is concerned it is not completely realized now. But, once published, it formed a goal which tempted successive generations. Unable to find funds for a school in every parish, the Sixteenth Century began at the top. The Scottish Universities were small and poor. They had been given all the officers and organs of the academic Middle Ages— chancellors, rectors, the form, at least, of several faculties. But in practice they taught little except Arts and Divinity. The Reformers recast them, finding (except at St. Andrews to begin with) the kind of organization which has become typical of Scottish university life, and which the Scottish example has passed on to other countries. It takes the form of a single college with a permanent principal and teachers who act in council with him. In a spirit of optimism, and rivalry between towns and nobles, three more college-universities were founded: only one of them, Edinburgh (1583), survives.

Repeated attempts were made in the Seventeenth Century to realize Knox's idea of a school in every parish. They were defeated, at first, by wars and ecclesiastical crises. At last, in 1696, when the Presbyterian Church of Scotland had been re-established, the Scots Estates passed the famous Act for the Settling of Schools, under which the landowners of each parish were to build a school (if one did not exist already) and to pay a schoolmaster not less than 100 or more than 200 merks per annum ($£5$, 11s. 1½d. to $£11$, 2s. 3d. sterling) raising the money by a local assessment. The real management of the schools, however, was in the hands of the Church, particularly of the parish ministers and of the presbyteries, who supervised the enforcement of the Act. The Parliament of Great Britain had little time and no money to give to Scottish education after 1707. It was not till 1803 that a second Act rather more than doubled the salaries of parish schoolmasters and ordered that they should be provided with houses of two rooms at least—described by angry landowners as 'palaces for dominies'.

Evidently there was nothing very magnificent about arrangements of this kind, beyond the fact that they did provide Scotland with something which no other European country possessed at the time—a system of schooling open to the majority of the people. The parish 'dominie' is a great figure in Scottish tradition, and rightly so, though modern writers on education, perhaps influenced by an entertaining but rather silly late-Victorian book, Graham's *Social Life in Scotland in the Eighteenth Century*, have been inclined to sneer at him. Even with school fees, which seldom amounted to more than 8s. a year for an older pupil, and small payments that often came to him as clerk to the kirk session and parish registrar, he was poor enough. But he was usually a man of real education who had spent some time at a university—quite often, indeed, a 'stickit minister' who had trained for the Church but, for some reason, had failed to reach the pulpit. Normally he could give what would now be called secondary education, besides reading, writing, and arithmetic. His pupils came to him each with a peat [1] under his arm to keep the school fire going, but they came, and it was traditional that, where they showed capacity for learning, he could carry them on to the university. Several generations passed before the Act of 1696 was fully applied and every parish had its school. Education was not compulsory, but it was general. Boys of all social classes went to the parish schools, at least for a year or two, and girls went too—co-education has been a normal thing in Scotland almost since the national system began, though the universities did not admit

[1] Peat is the dried turf of bogs, still used as fuel in the Highlands.

women till the Nineteenth Century. In large parishes, where some children could not reach the school beside the church, 'side schools' were established, and special schools were set up in the Highlands, largely as outposts of Protestant, Lowland 'civilization' among the often Roman Catholic Gaels. There was private enterprise in education too. Before the end of the Eighteenth Century innumerable 'adventure schools' taught reading and counting, sometimes higher subjects as well.

In the towns something like John Knox's proposed provision of 'colleges' grew up. Some of the burgh schools had existed from the Middle Ages or were taken over by town councils when monasteries or cathedral chapters ceased to be able to maintain them. It came to be recognized that each burgh should have a grammar school of some kind. In the late Eighteenth Century these were supplemented by 'academies', which taught mathematics, English, history and scientific subjects rather than Latin. Later, secondary schools of these two types were gradually merged with one another. 'Academy' became, and remains in most parts of Scotland, the commonest name for a school of some importance, whose head is usually called 'rector'.

It was in the Eighteenth Century that the Scottish universities began to have a great reputation in the world. They were still poor and the number of teachers was small, but included an extraordinary high proportion of famous names—William Robertson, the historian: Colin Maclaurin, the mathematician: Frances Hutcheson, Thomas Reid, Dugald Stewart, Adam Smith, philosophers: Joseph Black, the discoverer of latent heat: successive members of the Gregory family, mathematicians, astronomers, leaders in medicine: other founders of the medical schools of Edinburgh and Glasgow: in law the great Institutionalists and John Millar, constitutional theorist. Just before the century ended, the foundations of the first great technical institution in Britain, now the Royal College of Science and Technology, were laid when an enterprising but eccentric Glasgow professor, John Anderson, attempted to set up a second university there. Many students came to the Scots colleges from England and Ireland— chiefly nonconformists who could not be admitted to the Anglican universities, but also young men who wanted something beyond the narrowly classical learning of Oxford and Cambridge.

The Scottish educational system 150 years ago was still an ideal only partly fulfilled. Its parts were not properly co-ordinated. The only body which had some influence over all of them was the Church, to which all teachers from parish dominies to professors must belong: the General Assembly's Education Committee, which still exists, was the nearest thing to a central Education Department. But the ideal of schools open to all comers was a living one. The system was paid for and managed almost exclusively by Scotsmen. There was, indeed, very little of the formal provision for the maintenance of poor students that John Knox had looked for in 1560, though there were modest bursaries (scholarships) at the universities which might be won by pupils from the parish schools. Many poor boys of ability must have missed higher education altogether: indeed some scarcely got to school at all. The case of Robert Burns who, with less than three years' regular schooling and a few weeks spent under specialist teachers, had quite as good a knowledge of literature, mensuration and languages as many Scottish pupils of today's secondary schools, was no doubt unusual, but not very rare. The belief that schools were for people of all classes, that a clever boy ought to have his chance, was very widespread. To help such a boy, especially if his aim was to become a minister, was felt to be an act of virtue. In a country parish or small town his success was a source of local pride. The aims of education were clear in Scottish minds. They were to give learning and equipment either for membership of a literate church and society or for a profession, not 'adjustment to life' or the acquirement of habits and graces suitable to a governing class.

It was only in the second half of the Nineteenth Century that the British State began to control Scottish education. This was due partly to changes in England, where Parliament found it necessary first to subsidize schools and then to organize them, and partly to Disruption in the Scottish Church. In a sense, the Disruption helped education in Scotland. Many teachers joined the Free Church: David Stow, a Glasgow business man who had founded the first important training college, left the Church of Scotland, and all the college staff went with him. Partly to allow such people to continue their work, partly to assert itself as a national body, the Free Church set up its own schools and colleges. This was particularly useful in the spreading industrial towns, where the old system had broken down and there was a good deal of illiteracy. Once the Established Church had ceased to speak for the majority of Scots people, however, its control of education could scarcely continue for very long. With the Act of 1872, it was strongly curtailed.

This was a sequel to the Education Act of 1870, which, for the first time in England and Wales, established a uniform system of elementary schooling. The social effects of the Scottish Act were much less revolutionary: though it made education compulsory (which did not happen in England till eight years later) 80 per cent. of Scottish children between six and thirteen were already attending schools, and it seems safe to say that most of those who were not there had already learned to read and write or would have done so without compulsion. Already one child in 140 was attending a secondary school in Scotland, compared with one in 249 in Prussia, one in 570 in France, and one in 1300 in England.

The change in Scotland was in organization and finance, certainly important enough. For some time Scottish schools had been receiving their share of grants originally planned for England and Wales and supervised by the same Government agencies on both sides of the Border. Now much larger sums were provided and a separate Scotch Education Department was set up to regulate the whole system. An elected school board in each parish and burgh took control of the public schools—which, in Scotland, as in the United States, are schools open to all children. There was a very general interest in these councils. Unlike similar

English bodies they could deal with secondary education. They rebuilt the schools: probably the name of a parish board appears on at least half of the school buildings still used in Scotland. Largely through them the new Department unified the whole scheme of instruction outside the universities, which it did not control. Fees in elementary schools were abolished, 'free places' were provided in the secondary schools. Finally, in 1901, a Scots-American millionaire, Andrew Carnegie, set up a trust for the Scottish Universities with funds large enough to pay the university fees of all poor students.

It could be said, at this stage, that the programme of 1560 had almost been realized. There was simple schooling for every child and an opportunity of something more for almost all who were fit to take it. If one looks at these things with the eyes of a traditional Scot, what has followed since has been a smoothing and completion of the system on one side and a striking departure from it on the other. In many secondary schools fees disappeared after 1918: after 1945 only a handful of what are oddly called 'fee-paying schools' was left. Grants and bursaries were provided to maintain young people whose parents were not too prosperous at secondary schools and universities. Most important, perhaps (though this certainly does not accord with any idea of John Knox's), the Roman Catholic schools, which were independent and had little support from the taxes before 1918, have been brought into the general system without losing their special character: here Scotland set an example which other countries have followed with some difficulty, if at all.

It is almost true now, as it certainly never has been in the past, that no Scotsman earning less than a reasonable middle-class income need make any real sacrifice to educate his child. Yet, in fact, such sacrifices are being made, perhaps with more strain and anxiety than at any time in the last half century or more. Till recent years the Scottish public schools were generally felt to be good enough for anybody, at least so far as book-learning was concerned. It is true that in the Nineteenth Century, the sons of the country gentry, who had once sat under the parish dominies before going to an academy or high school in one of the cities, began to be sent to the great public schools in England, and from there to Oxford or Cambridge. Half a dozen boarding schools on the English pattern were even founded in Scotland itself. Edinburgh had (and has) a group of specially famous endowed schools. In other towns well-to-do parents were prepared to pay a little more than other people for a kind of schooling, private or public in either sense of the word, that seemed likely to give their children some sense of social privilege. But, in general, public education was for all in Scotland, just as it is in the United States, but certainly never has been in England. Scots people were convinced, and certainly not without some reason, that, on its own principles, their national system led the world.

They are not too sure of that now. For the public schools have taken a turn which many Scotsmen find it hard to understand. Perhaps it may be said that the system which grew out of John Knox's programme seemed good enough for all because it aimed so insistently at making the best of the best, according to its own standards. Implicitly it favoured *la carrière ouverte aux talents*: though there was very little equality of opportunity for all classes in the Scotland of 1560 or even 1696, the well-schooled son of a peasant could at least go as far as sheer intelligence would take him. But while the public schools made for equality in this sense they never pretended that all could be equal in book-learning, which was their business. People who can get little out of books may, indeed, be better and more useful men and women than university graduates are, but once they had got from the schools what they could reasonably be expected to absorb neither the parish dominie nor the academy rector had much interest in them: in the words of the first *Buke of Discipline* 'they must be sent to some handicraft or some other profitable exercise'. The crowning work of the schools was to teach the 'lad o' pairts' or the girl who could equal him.

There may be a certain narrowness in this point of view, but it is at least an intelligible one—a natural one too for educationists who have always wished, and still wish, that most (or all) of their teachers should be university graduates.[1] But among the policy-makers of Scottish education faith in such values has been growing weaker for half a century. Their tendency has been to concentrate attention not on the cleverest children but on those who could get less out of book-learning, and

---

[1] Graduates or not, Scottish teachers must all pass through a recognized training college.

consequently to think more about other things than books—about the feeding, clothing, and comfort of their pupils, about what would interest and amuse children who could not see much reason for staying in school at all.

This reaction could have been a healthy one. The ideal of schooling for all and higher education for those who were fit for it had been fairly fully achieved: it was not unreasonable to look for something more. While Scottish instruction has been competent, it has sometimes seemed to turn out too many people who knew their books without enjoying or understanding them very thoroughly: from this point of view even the educators have not always been very fully educated. It is very true, also, that children who are cold, underfed or under-exercised will not learn so easily as healthy and comfortable ones. Scottish education might have flowered if it had given more thought to such things without losing its standards.

Unluckily it had to meet other influences just when it was growing a little uncertain of itself. One was an idea of democracy which insisted not only that men should be equal before the law and should have an equal chance of developing their talents but also that their talents were bound to be equally valuable and equally suitable for encouragement in the schools. If this was so, it was the weakest, not the ablest, who deserved most of a teacher's attention and the State's. Then there came the years of economic depression when there was nothing for older children to do outside the schools except 'blind alley jobs' which left them unemployed at sixteen. Finally there was the appearance of a new sort of authority controlling the schools.

The old school boards, successors to the church in the management of education in each parish, disappeared in 1918. They had been successful and had attracted a good many members with a special interest in education, but in England schooling was organized by counties, and so it must be in Scotland too. At first there were specially elected education authorities for the shires and large cities, but these, too, were swept away in 1929, when education committees of county and city councils, more or less on the English model, took control of a system that was already much more highly centralized under the Scottish Department than it had once been. The education committees have members who represent the churches and sometimes men or women specially co-opted. But it can happen that the majority, elected as town or county councillors, have very little interest in learning and, indeed, not much experience of it beyond the 'three Rs'. Health services, milk and meals, and the ideal of complete equality among children whatever their intelligence may be, can appeal more to such authorities than any question of what, or how much, shall actually be learned at school. Such things may be left, very largely, to directors of education, whose point of view can sometimes be fairly close to that of the committees who appointed them.

In the workless 1930s, when it seemed to many that the first need was 'to keep the children off the streets' both committee men and teachers learnt to feel that the first reform must be the raising of the school leaving age—a step towards social equality which would bring with it 'secondary education for all'. Though by law this step could have been taken in Scotland alone, it was scarcely possible to make such a change before 1939. Treasury grants for Scottish education were fixed on the basis of eleven-eighteiths of what was spent by the Ministry of Education in England, and Scotland already provided a far higher proportion of secondary school places than English education committees did, most of them without fees.

One result of such a state of things (now to be changed in a way still uncertain) has been that Scotland could afford fewer teachers. In theory, classes in primary schools should not have more than thirty-five pupils or those in secondary schools more than thirty. But in fact the limits often have to be disregarded. A spokesman for the Educational Institute of Scotland, the leading organization of teachers, has claimed that more than half the school classes were overcrowded in 1957. When the leaving age was raised to fifteen after the war years, during which no building or re-equipment had been possible, there was a serious shortage of classrooms and teachers, even of desks, school books and writing paper. In these circumstances the new plans for secondary education made a difficult start. There were to be schools of two types—senior secondary, which could give 'academic' education, of the established kind, and junior secondary for those who meant to leave at fifteen and could be 'educated for life' rather than for examinations. All children must leave their primary schools before they were twelve, whether they had passed an examination which could prove them literate or not.

These arrangements have had social effects, some of which were no doubt unexpected. In the countryside they have killed the tradition of the parish school where children could find all the learning they needed. There is some form of secondary education for all, perhaps, but there are far fewer centres of secondary teaching in Scotland today than there were a century ago. Most country children must leave their villages, glens or islands for a neighbouring town (some of them must be away from home for weeks on end); and all this not necessarily to get knowledge which is going to be particularly useful for them but to sit through junior secondary classes the purpose and value of which is not always very clear either to their parents or to themselves. In all parts of Scotland parents do, in fact, tend to prefer the 'academic' type of secondary schooling if their children can qualify themselves for it. The result is that the lower classes of senior secondary schools are crowded. 'Comprehensive' schools may offer both types of secondary learning, but it is not clear that this is likely to end a state of things in which scores of thousands embark on a course which should last six years, but only some 20 per cent. of them finish it. The crown of the completed course was once a national Leaving Certificate, given after an examination planned with real intelligence (it avoided set books) by the Scottish Education Department. To avoid discouraging the less 'academic', however, this certificate is now given to pupils who have passed in a single subject, which may be Lower Homecraft. Naturally, it has lost some of its value, and there is a movement to replace it with a two-tier examination similar to the English General Certificate of Education.

In fact, many of the distinctive features of the national system seem to be disappearing. There is, of course, a Youth Service, as in England, and various devices or projects for part-time schooling after fifteen for those who leave then. But the Scottish public schools tend to take on a proletarian character such as has always attached itself to 'council' schooling in England, though it is, perhaps, growing weaker there now. As things are at present, most of the time and energy of Scottish secondary teachers (to say nothing of the money that goes into school building) must be spent on children who are never going to complete the work before them. There is the less to spare for really able boys and girls. The teaching of science has suffered particularly badly.

Inevitably, parents who can manage to pay for a type of school where the idea of a complete secondary education can be taken more seriously are anxious to do so, as many of them never were in the past. The number of schools for which fees can still be paid, whether they are independent or run by local councils, has fallen since the war. But the demand for places in them has soared. It would not be true to say that the anxious worry of parents who want to see their children pass into 'a good school' is quite as great as it is in England. The fear that children must drop into a lower social class if they fail in an entrance test is less deep.

But, for the first time in history the Scottish public school system is beginning to seem a second best to parents who have no family tradition of education outside it. Nearly all the schools which charge fees receive grants from the State. Their fees are often low enough, but they serve the purpose of ensuring that the education these schools give is thought to be worth paying for. It is because they represent the old national habit of thorough book-learning rather than because they can sometimes be made to seem, socially, to be a little like English Public Schools that the pressure for places in them is now so strong.

Evidently the Scottish national system is at a turning point. Most primary teaching is still notably thorough. It is still true that boys and girls from public secondary schools can hope to rise as far as their ability will take them. Scotland sends one in 348 of its young people to the universities: this compares with one in 639 for England. The Scottish universities are constantly developing new departments and new professorships. Directly or indirectly, they now depend almost entirely on public funds, though the grant for each student in Scotland is still below the United Kingdom average. Specialist colleges of technology, art, agriculture, music, and commerce have expanded, and the standards of teaching in some of them are very high.

But the time could come fairly quickly and easily when the principle that the most must be made of the best mental ability, from whatever sort of home it may come, would be much more seriously weakened than it has yet been. Too often, perhaps, people in authority at the universities have no personal experience of the tradition they have to work in—do not understand, for example, a system which has always aimed at a fairly wide and general education, both at school and later, rather than at severe specialization. It seems unfortunate that Scotland does not supply more of her own university teachers. Ours is the first generation in which two of the four university principals have been educated outside Scotland: the proportion of professors and lecturers in some faculties who come to their work with a direct knowledge of the Scottish tradition is no higher.

Scottish education has one other weakness, unexpected in a system which has been fully national for nearly three centuries. It is apt to be too little aware of its own national roots. No doubt this has happened partly because, through most of this time, there has been no national State in Scotland.

In the days before European governments began to control the schools, children were taught little about their own countries, their own language, literature, music. Boys learned more in school about the history of the Jews, Greeks and Romans than about the past of the land they belonged to—France, England, Germany. This sort of knowledge was to be gathered at the fireside or from private reading. It was in those days that Scottish education formed its habits. When national systems of schooling grew up in other countries the study of national subjects grew with them. The British State, however, was not passionately interested in Scottish history, literature or language—in providing Scottish children with the kind of knowledge which helps peoples to understand themselves and the present through the things which their past has given them. Our educationists are still apt to assume that these are matters which can be picked up outside school; or, at least, need be taught only to very young children. Teachers are, indeed, recommended officially not to forget them, but the Scottish examination system has not made their study necessary, or even rewarding. Something about Scotland's past is taught in primary schools, and often Scots songs and ballads too. But it is sometimes quite possible for a student to take an honours degree in History without reading a book or answering a question about Scotland, and the fact that most subjects which have a French, English or American aspect also have a Scottish one is scarcely appreciated. Perhaps it is because of this that history of any kind is less studied in Scots schools and universities than in most others, though it is a subject which has always interested Scottish people.

In recent years there have been some protests against the failure to teach Scots children more about their own land and people. 'Unless the schools learn to make a place for national culture here, as they do in other countries, it is bound to weaken still further', declared the report of a Saltire Society committee, *Scotland in the Schools* (1953). 'If it were dead there would seem to be very little future for Scottish nationality or for Scottish education as an independent system. As a force making for general literacy this system has pretty well accomplished its task. Its achievement in that direction is high, but no longer very noticeably higher than that of other and younger national systems. The Scot need—and indeed can—no longer feel that but for his luck in being born North of the Border he might scarcely have been able to read or write, to get a secondary education or attend a university. . . . The one thing which Scottish schools can do for him, and no others can attempt, is to give him an understanding of his own national background, of the life he lives and the towns and countrysides he knows. And it is precisely on this side that the Scottish educational tradition is weakest.' Unluckily Scottish teachers themselves are often not well equipped for this work. Like men of some other small nations, Scots (Scottish Nationalists included) are apt to take an internationalist view of the world. One would like to think this a virtue, but, particularly among those who were students in the 1930s, there are a good many teachers who have persuaded themselves that if they are to be truly enlightened and open-minded they must cease to feel and think as Scots. This is a real obstacle to the sort of change in educational outlook which the Saltire Society's report asked for, and without which (it suggested) 'we must expect either a root or branch reform of the whole national system of education or its replacement by an organization and methods borrowed directly from England, or perhaps from the United States'.

Chapter Six

SCOTLAND IN LAW

'IN a sense since the Union with England in 1707, Scotland as a nation has survived in and through her laws and legal system', writes Professor T. B. Smith in his valuable work on the development of Scots law.[1] No doubt this is very much a lawyer's view. There are certainly Scotsmen little concerned with the law who scarcely feel it to be a main part of their national life, yet most of them are pleased to think that their country has a unique legal structure of its own.

The existence of this system is, indeed, an astonishing thing, and its influence on the Scottish people in the last three centuries has probably been deeper than is often realized. Though there are dozens of law-making bodies at work in the English-speaking world, the basis and framework of the law in most states of the American Union and the British Commonwealth is fairly uniform. It is the common law of England. North of the Tweed, however, this uniformity ceases. There has been no Scottish legislature for more than 250 years, yet the whole legal system remains distinct, both the courts and many of the laws they administer. It is the boast of Scots lawyers that their system combines the qualities

[1] *The British Commonwealth: the Development of its Laws and Constitution*, edited by George W. Keeton. Vol. 1, pp. 603–1137.

of Anglo-American law, which has built itself upon precedents and parliamentary enactments rather than on general rules, with those of Continental European systems, which have their roots in the law of Rome and have tried to deduce from it principles fit to govern all law-making. Scots and English law are certainly closer to one another than they were a century ago, but the fundamental differences between them are still almost as obvious as they were then.

The lowest courts in the two countries look very much alike. Both have unpaid justices of the peace. But though there have been Scottish J.P.s since 1587, they have never had the importance that they still hold in England. Of course an enormous number of small offences and claims are dealt with in magistrates' courts, but these are busiest in the towns, and there the judges are not J.P.s but bailies, who are chosen by the burgh councils from among their own members, and, like other councillors, can hold this place only if the voters re-elect them. As in the United States, judges who depend on a popular vote can have special difficulties to face, but the bailie means more to Scotsmen than the Justice of the Peace.

By far the most important of local courts, however, is the sheriff's. It can deal with all crimes except the highest—treason, murder, rape, incest and a few others —and with a very wide range of civil cases. In the Middle Ages the sheriff was the chief royal official in a county. He still has some administrative duties: for instance, he is the presiding officer at parliamentary elections. But all sheriffs are professional lawyers.

Scotland is divided nowadays into twelve sheriffdoms. Each has a sheriff principal, who hears appeal from its courts. He is not, however, a full-time judge, except in the sheriffdoms that embrace Glasgow and Edinburgh. The work of the sheriff courts is done mainly by sheriffs substitute, appointed for life by the Crown. When he is dealing with serious crime the sheriff substitute sits with a jury of fifteen. The heaviest sentence he can give is one of two years' imprisonment. Where it seems likely that this will not be severe enough the prisoner is sent to the High Court. Both the sheriff's powers and the range of his work, however, are formidable. Most of the cases which, in England, would go to quarter-sessions, a recorder or a county court judge, go to him, besides many which would go to the English High Court. In each of the four cities there are several sheriffs substitute, and sheriff courts are held in almost every town of importance and in country districts where there is no large town.

Above them are the Supreme Courts of Scotland. The judges are the fifteen Senators of the College of Justice. The other members of this august but not corporately active body are the advocates (*anglicé*, barristers) who practise before them and an ancient body of solicitors, the Writers to the Signet. Like the sheriffs, all the Senators deal with both civil and criminal cases. For the first they are Lords of Council and Session, and sit in the Court of Session, which meets only in Edinburgh. Changing their maroon robes for scarlet and white, they are also Lords Commissioners of Justiciary, and may go on circuit to try criminal cases in various towns from Inverness to Dumfries, or sit in Edinburgh for local criminal trials and for appeals. For these purposes they form the High Court of Justiciary.

Each of them is a lord for life: in the Eighteenth Century and earlier, when every judge had landed possessions of some kind, this title was linked with the name of his estate, as it sometimes is still. Till our own century a Lord of Session's wife did not formally share her husband's title. This did not matter very much in the days when the wife of Mr. Broun of Blacktoun was always spoken of in Scotland as 'Leddy Blacktoun'.[1] But misunderstanding was apt to arise when Lord Blacktoun, a distinguished jurist, arrived at a hotel, or even a palace, outside Scotland, accompanied by Mrs. Broun; and since 1905 every judge's wife is, officially, a lady.

The picturesque trimmings of the Scottish legal system are proof enough in themselves that it has a long history behind it. The High Court of Justiciary has evolved from the court of the medieval Justiciars, supreme judges of Scotland after the king—who, from time to time, would hold his own justice-ayres. Its head, the Lord Justice-General, represents the ancient Justiciar himself. In the Twelfth and Thirteenth Centuries, when Justiciars dealt with important cases of many kinds, the law they administered was largely Anglo-Norman. It had replaced (or sometimes absorbed) the ancient Celtic customs of the country. After the

[1] And when Scotswomen kept their maiden surnames in practice after marriage, as they still do in law.

War of Independence, however, the Scots courts ceased to borrow from England, though old Anglo-Norman law books were still used. Young Scots studied not at Oxford, Cambridge, or the London Inns of Court, but at Continental universities.

For some time the law of Scotland seems to have been in a very unsettled state. The Scots Parliament passed some useful and enlightened Acts in the Fifteenth Century and later, which showed a notable concern for those who, in many other European countries, would still have been serfs—'the puir people that laubouris the grund'. A system of free legal aid for poor litigants has existed in Scotland since 1424. It still functions in criminal cases, where the new system of 'assisted litigation' introduced in 1949 has not yet been applied. But even good laws could do little when most courts were feudal ones whose judges might have scarcely any legal training. Two processes of reform worked to overcome this weakness. The first sought for new royal courts, committees of the King's council or the Parliament, to which appeals could be taken. The second was the Reception of the Roman Law, which came strongly into Scotland in the Fifteenth Century and later in a form borrowed from the great Continental commentators by young men who learned to know them first in Italy and France, then (after the Reformation) chiefly in Holland. Most of the early professional lawyers in Scotland were churchmen and canon law has left its mark on the Scottish system.

The first of these movements culminated in the founding of the Court of Session (1532), and the existence of this supreme civil appeal court, with its corps of learned legal practitioners, stimulated the second movement, which gave Scots law its form.

Today's Court of Session, which sits, appropriately enough, in the old Parliament House of Scotland, is a complicated structure. It consists of two houses, Outer and Inner. The judges of the Outer House (Lords Ordinary) deal with cases which come directly to the court either because they seem too important for the sheriffs or (as with divorce actions) because no other court can try them. The Inner House has two Divisions. The head of the First Division is the Lord President of the Court of Session, who is also Lord Justice-General. The head of the Second is the Lord Justice-Clerk. Both these bodies deal mainly with appeals, from the sheriff courts or from decisions of the Outer House. Yet in an important sense the Court remains one. Difficult questions can be brought before all the judges sitting together, or before seven or five of them. It is in this way that many of the rules of Scots law have been worked out and established. Such sittings have a special authority. Perhaps it is true to say that they have been particularly useful when an Act of the British Parliament or a decision of the House of Lords as an appeal court has seemed to contradict the principles of the law of Scotland.

For, though the Session is called a supreme court, appeals against its decisions can, in fact, go to the House of Lords in London. Since the Treaty of Union seems to safeguard the independence of the Scottish courts—indeed, of the whole legal system—this is an odd state of affairs: indeed it is very doubtful whether it does not break the bargain on which the United Kingdom is founded. There is no appeal out of Scotland in criminal matters: the Scottish Criminal Appeal Court, set up in 1926, is in fact an augmented sitting of the High Court of Justiciary itself, very useful in settling difficult questions as well as in giving an assurance of justice in doubtful cases. Scottish criminal law has remained for the most part a native growth, seldom deeply altered by Acts of the British Parliament. Its principles are simple and clear. The law in civil cases, on the other hand, has had to adapt itself to the decisions of judges in London who, for many decades, scarcely pretended to understand it. The comment of Lord Chancellor Erskine (1750–1823), a Scot by birth, but an English lawyer, was not untypical: 'I know something of the law, but of Scotch law I am as ignorant as a native of Mexico'.

The influence of English judges who found a system different from their own alarming or unintelligible undoubtedly prompted the British Parliament to make changes which were not at all welcome in Edinburgh— to establish a Scottish Court of Exchequer on the English model and to introduce jury trials in some civil cases. The Exchequer Court, like the old Scottish Court of Admiralty, has been absorbed by the Court of Session. Civil juries are unpopular, not least with the jurors, all of whom must be drawn from the neighbourhood of Edinburgh. They ceased during the war of 1939–45, and may be allowed to disappear altogether now that Englishmen themselves are discovering that, however useful a jury may be in protecting people accused of crime, it can be a very poor safeguard of money or rights in disputes between one man and another.

The Court of Session has been better protected since 1876, when it became usual to have at least one Scottish judge in the House of Lords. By custom there are now two Scottish Lords of Appeal in London, who can do something to ensure that the principles of Scots law are understood by those who have to deal with them there. It is surprising enough, however, that the system should have kept its individuality for so many generations— under Governments who cared nothing for it and a supreme appeal court to which it was a mystery. It is more than surprising that, after 1707, Scots law should have enlarged and completed itself almost without the help of a law-making Parliament.

For this is what happened in the Eighteenth Century and the early Nineteenth. The law of Scotland was developing very rapidly before the Union. The confusion of the centuries when most courts were feudal and most judges very little learned in the law may perhaps have had one useful result. It may have been partly to meet the needs of such judges that the forms of procedure in Scotland were simplified just when, under professional judges in England, they were growing more elaborate, and that lawyers learned to depend on principles rather than on the precedents set by previous decisions of the courts—decisions which, under the conditions of that day, would scarcely be collected, compared and studied. It was because it supplied such principles that Roman law, as interpreted by generations of Continental jurists, was eagerly welcomed in Scotland, but it was never the only law recognized by Scottish courts. Feudal law, church law, ancient customs, and (of course) the Acts of Scots Parliaments also had authority. What is called the common law of Scotland is drawn from all these sources. The late Lord Cooper, President of the Court of Session, was able to declare that it was this law, rather than statutes of United Kingdom Parliaments, which still regulated and defined 'all the main rights and duties of the Scottish citizen'.[1]

But three centuries ago that system had still to be made. It was the work of lawyers who, in books that are still authoritative, laid down the lines of its development. The greatest of these was Viscount Stair, whose *Institutions of the Law of Scotland* was published in 1681. Law, for him, was 'reason itself as it is versant about the rights of man'. It was he who fused together the varying strains of materials which have gone to make the body of Scots law. 'The fact that we in Scotland', wrote Sir Archibald Campbell Black, 'possess a system of law based upon the philosophic method of starting with a right and ending with a vindication is attributable to the genius of Stair'.[2] All other Institutional writers have followed him, and his book is still quoted, not only in Scottish courts.

Stair was only nine years dead when the Scots State and its Parliament ceased to exist. His work was

[1] *The Scottish Legal Tradition*, a Saltire pamphlet, 1949.
[2] In *Sources and Literature of Scots Law* (Stair Society 1936).

continued, however, by John Erskine (1695–1768), by David Hume, nephew of the philosopher, whose *Commentaries* on the criminal law appeared in 1797, and by George Joseph Bell (1770–1843) whose work on mercantile law may be said to have completed the classical Scots system. Each of the last three was, in his day, Professor of Scots Law at Edinburgh. In Scotland legal training belongs to the universities. But scholarship alone could not have made the system. It has depended for its development on the corporate spirit of practising lawyers, above all of judges and advocates, who, working on the principles set out by the Institutionalists, have set themselves to find an adequate legal solution for the changing problems of their times.

No doubt this kind of thing can have its dangers, neatly summarized in the boast of Lord Justice-Clerk Braxfield, the most notorious, though one of the ablest, of Scottish criminal judges—'Bring me the prisoner and I'll find the law'. Lord Braxfield, who dominated the trials of political reformers in the days of the French Revolution and is the original of R. L. Stevenson's Weir of Hermiston, was able to develop the rather uncertain law of sedition in a way very welcome to the government of the younger Pitt. He would scarcely have been so well-remembered if Scots judges who used their power oppressively had been less rare. The development of the law has never depended on individual judges alone.

The idea that courts must be bound by the precedent of earlier decisions has a very much smaller part in Scottish legal thinking than in English. The influence of the House of Lords has tended to impose this idea on

Scotland, but it is possible for the Supreme Courts to reverse unsuitable precedents of their own by holding special sittings, and the view of a recognized Institutional writer may overrule that of any single judge. To Scotsmen the thought that any branch of the law can safely be allowed to be less than equitable has always been a strange one. What is called the *nobile officium* of the courts, particularly the Court of Session, has been used to supply defects as they appeared. Formally it is certainly less important now than it once was. The courts' powers of interpretation have been limited by some statutes. But Scots lawyers are usually reluctant to believe that a new problem of their profession must be left to the decision of Parliament: they are apt to feel that the courts ought to be able to find a way of doing justice—if necessary of working out a new principle which can be applied in the future.

The Faculty of Advocates, which includes all who practise at the bar of the Supreme Courts, has had, and still has, a powerful influence on Scottish life and law. Since political life of a normally constructive kind ceased to be possible in Scotland, it has attracted a remarkable number of educated and intelligent men, who must understand their country's habits and some of its problems, and are bound, in the nature of things, to try to ensure that the legal system is as respected and as practically useful as they can make it. The Law Society of Scotland, to which all solicitors (formerly law agents or writers) must now belong, has a similar interest.

Scots law could scarcely have existed for so long as a separate system if the people of Scotland had no preferred it for practical reasons as well as patriotic ones. It has lived under the shadow of the law of England, which has conquered one new country after another and has been perfectly capable of embracing Scotland too if Scots could be persuaded to ask for it. The sheer pressure of this (more or less latent) competition may have had something to do with the vigour and adaptability of Scots law, some of whose features have been imitated, more or less consciously, by English lawmakers.

In Scotland, practically all criminal prosecutions have been in the hands of the Crown, as more and more of them have come to be in England. They are controlled by the Lord Advocate, who is both a member of the Government and himself chief public prosecutor. His senior assistant is the Solicitor-General for Scotland, also a minister. Then there are Advocates Depute, who may appear for the Crown in the High Court; and, in the lower courts, Procurators-fiscal with whom the Lord Advocate deals through the Crown Office. There are no coroner's courts in Scotland and no public preliminary hearings before magistrates in criminal cases. A prisoner is formally committed for trial by the sheriff and examined privately by the procurator-fiscal under conditions which give him all possible protection. Thus a man accused of murder is in no danger of being tried publicly three times over as, in Scottish eyes, seems to happen under the English system; and the jury which finally deals with him can come to the case without prejudice.

Through Acts of Parliament English lawyers have recently tried to borrow the idea of diminished responsibility, which can prevent a conviction for murder, and the system by which men who fail to maintain their families can have the money due under a court order deducted from their wages instead of being sent to prison for debt. In both cases the borrowing seems to have met with some resistance. Divorce was possible in Scotland for nearly three centuries before it became a normal part of English law: in spite of this the Scottish divorce rate, though it has risen in recent years, is well below that of most English-speaking countries. Since the very early days of the Scottish system it has been almost impossible for a man to disinherit his wife and children completely, as an Englishman could do until 1938. There has been legal aid for the poor for more than five centuries, and the system is still more complete than it is in England.

In general, Scots law inclines to mercy both in practice and in form—to put the rights of the individual before the claims of the State. Capital offences were rare a century and a half ago when they were common in England, and executions for murder are rare now: there was none in the sixteen years before 1945. Scots kings were sometimes sued successfully in their own courts: that has been impossible since the Union, but Scotsmen have always been able to sue the Crown in contract. It could be argued that a Scotsman belongs to himself rather than to the State: he is free to commit suicide. He cannot be convicted of any crime without the corroborative evidence of at least two witnesses. This is a rule which undoubtedly complicates the work of prosecuting lawyers, yet the number of serious offences is not high. In every case the defender has the last word before the judge's summing-up.

Not only the rights of the accused (*scoticè* the pannel) but the consciences of individual jurors are protected. Since a jury's decision can be given by a majority there is no danger that members who do not agree with it may, in effect, be persuaded to perjure themselves. In a sense the Scots verdict of 'not proven' also protects a jury which strongly doubts a prisoner's innocence but does not feel able to convict him. It does not seem entirely unjust that an accused person who escapes merely because of some failure of evidence should not leave the court 'without a stain on his character'.

The law of Scotland is still, in the main, very satisfactory to Scotsmen. Lord Cooper was able to quote, with pride, the opinion of a French jurist, Professor Levy Ullman, that 'Scots Law, as it stands, gives us a picture of what will some day be the law of the civilized nations—namely a combination between the Anglo-Saxon system and the Continental system'. In the mid-Twentieth Century, however, it faces serious difficulties. The flood of new legislation and the setting up of administrative tribunals through which Government departments sometimes seem able to pass judgement on themselves are perhaps no more damaging in Scotland than elsewhere. But Acts of the British Parliament and decisions of the House of Lords sometimes seem to pay too little attention to Scottish legal principles. When Acts are made for the United Kingdom they are drawn in English terms: clauses which try to apply these terms to Scotland by translating them into the language of Scots Law are often inadequate or confusing. On the other hand, a Parliament in London has little time to spare for laws meant for Scotland alone.

The feudal land law of Scotland, for example, is, in many ways, a highly ingenious structure, remarkably well suited to days of active private enterprise. Among other things, it allowed the development of an estate to be planned intelligently, for example, while giving the developers almost all the advantages of free-hold ownership. A government which understood these principles might have adapted them to modern times, instead of by-passing them when it wanted to control the use of land, as modern governments have done: after all, under feudalism, all land is ultimately held of the Crown. But, as things stand, a good deal of Scottish land law, and certainly the law of heritage (inheritance of land) is over-complicated and out of date. Some detailed plans for reform exist, but no British government can find time to deal with them. It is complained that the simple rules of Scots law about a landowner's liability for accidents on his property have been complicated by House of Lords decisions on English principles, that the English law itself has since been simplified, but that Parliament cannot be persuaded to restore the old Scots system on this point. The legal status of women was once comparatively high in Scotland. In other countries it has been brought into line with modern social conditions, but here it has been found impossible to change arrangements which are not yet quite intolerable. Codification of Scots Law would have been natural and useful more than a century ago, but it could scarcely be carried through then by a Parliament to which the whole subject was strange, and it is just as unattainable today.

It may be necessary to the management of Scotland that most important legal appointments should have a political side to them. Almost every modern Lord President and Lord Justice-Clerk has been Lord Advocate or Solicitor-General in a party Government, and other appointments usually go to members of the party in power. This certainly helps to ensure that eminent Scots lawyers know something about the business of law-making in London. It can be said, too, that there is very little sign of party feeling in the administration of the law—opinion among advocates would react very badly to anything of that kind. But the need to qualify in party politics for legal promotion cannot always be a very healthy thing.

'Law is the reflection of the spirit of a people', wrote Lord Cooper, 'and so long as the Scots are conscious that they are a people they must preserve their law.' The survival and growth of the Scottish system under the Union is certainly a very remarkable fact, but it is at least doubtful how long its separate existence can continue. Professor Dewar Gibb has recorded[1] a conversation with Lord Cooper in which this greatest of recent Scots judges declared that Scotland's law and institutions must, in fact, be merged with England's unless Scotsmen won control of their own law-making. Many Scots lawyers certainly feel that the death of their system would be a loss not only to Scotland but to the world.

[1] *Saltire Review*, Summer, 1957.

Chapter Seven

THE MANAGEMENT OF SCOTLAND

IN this second half of the Twentieth Century Scotland is nearer to having the administrative framework of a distinct government of her own than she has been since 1707. Most of the work which, in England and Wales, is done by the Home Office and the Ministries of Health, Housing, Education, and Agriculture, is controlled for Scotland by one Cabinet Minister, the Secretary of State. The Lord Chancellor's functions as Minister of Justice in England are performed, in the main, by the Secretary of State, the Lord Advocate and the Lord President of the Court of Session. So far as Scottish roads are concerned, the Secretary of State is also Minister of Transport. In general, the Secretary of State for Scotland's four departments—Home, Health, Education, and Agriculture—cover most of the domestic business of government so far as it is not concerned with general economics.

In addition, he is a co-ordinator. Departments which act for the whole of Great Britain—Board of Trade, Post Office, Ministries of Labour, Supply, Power, Works, National Insurance—have Scottish offices of their own, each under a senior official. With these the Secretary of State has some contact, recognizable, though not too sharply defined. He is (or may seem to be) a sort of shadow-premier with a little cabinet of subordinate ministers. In addition to the two law officers there are now a Minister of State and three Parliamentary Joint Under-Secretaries, each of whom has some special responsibility for a Scottish Department.

This is, in the strictest sense, an extraordinary system by British, even by world-wide, standards. Perhaps Irish government before 1921 comes nearest to it. With its Lord Lieutenant and Chief Secretary, its separate legal structure and educational arrangements, Ireland when it was part of the United Kingdom stood a little as Scotland does now, in administrative form if not in practical fact. Not, however, as Scotland did then, for in 1921 this Scottish system was only half developed. It is in the main the growth of one long lifetime. One may add that Ireland had in its separate Privy Council the remains, or the germ, of a body with some emergency powers of legislation or of truly independent executive decision. Nothing of this sort has existed in Scotland since 1708. Here we have an administration entirely dependent on the Cabinet and Parliament of the United Kingdom.

Yet this is surprising fruit for a Treaty of Union which, two and a half centuries ago, seemed meant to be so far-reaching that, under it, the very names of the two uniting kingdoms might be expected to disappear. The truth is, perhaps, that politically Scotland and England in 1707 were much more unlike than they appeared to be. Perhaps it is natural for historians to argue that the two countries were bound to come together. They were neighbours, they had shared the same royal family for a century, both were Protestant, each was ruled (more or less) by a parliament, there had been many plans for uniting them. Inevitable or not, however, the Union was a direct reversal of the main course of Scottish history, which had been filled with the struggle to assert the country's freedom. Certainly it was not love of the Scots which led English statesmen to insist on an 'incorporating union' rather than the sort of federal link which tied together the Dutch provinces or the Swiss cantons: what they looked for was an absolute safeguard against a second Restoration of the Roman Catholic Stewarts in Scotland. There cannot be much doubt that with most Scotsmen the Union was intensely unpopular, though Presbyterian Whigs, Jacobites who were largely Episcopalian or Roman Catholic, and plain patriots like Andrew Fletcher of Saltoun, were not able to unite against it. In the circumstances it was not surprising if neither side was really very anxious to make the change more sweeping and complete in practice than was absolutely necessary. The Treaty does, in fact, consist very largely of clauses which were intended to safeguard Scottish institutions against any sudden change. It has been argued, by the late Lord Cooper among others, that there was a fundamental difference between the Parliament of England, which was sovereign, and the Scots Parliament (the Estates of Scotland), which was not. Certainly the Government of England (king, lords, and commons together) concentrated all authority in itself as no Scottish Government ever could.

Scotland in 1707 was a feudal country: this meant, in practice, that the government had no system of administration which could impose its will without question. We talk loosely of English feudalism, and think of the Justices of the Peace who administered the counties besides acting as unpaid judges in the lesser courts. Most of the English J.P.s were squires, but they were appointed by the Crown and could be removed. Their legal powers did not come to them by inheritance as those of Scottish lairds did.

The Scots Crown's chief representative in the shire was the sheriff, both judge and administrator, but in 1707 most sheriffs held their office by hereditary right. Important landowners, holders of baronies and regalities, had courts and administrative powers of their own over which the Crown had scarcely any control. The Scottish Parliament itself was a feudal assembly. In a sense quite unfamiliar to us it was completely representative. Almost every acre of land had its spokesman— Lord of Parliament or elected commissioner—but there was, strictly speaking, no representation of people. The only electors in the shires (with a very few exceptions) were the Crown's tenants-in-chief: it was their feudal status which gave them the vote.

Even the towns were feudal units. The royal burghs, the only towns represented in the Estates, held their place there as corporate tenants-in-chief of the Crown, just as the peers and voters in the shires were individual freeholders. These royal burghs were of all sizes, from the merest villages to the capital city of Edinburgh. Many of them, like Edinburgh itself, had grown up or been founded by the kings beside royal castles. Others, like Glasgow, were the creations of bishops or abbots and had gradually grown in importance until they had to be received into the Convention of Royal Burghs, a sort of sub-parliament for municipal affairs which continued to deal with many questions of trade even after the Union. It still exists, one of the oldest representative bodies in the world, though it has lost a good deal of its old importance and includes towns which have never had any royal privilege. But 250 years ago the burgh councils were very definitely privileged bodies, renewing themselves by co-option from the members of other privileged groups, the guilds of merchants and craftsmen. The chief counter-influence to this structure of feudalism and privilege was not the government but the Church. In every parish the kirk session, chosen from and (at least indirectly) by the people, controlled not only ecclesiastical affairs but poor relief and other social activities, and had a hand in education: it may even be said to have provided the only effective police force. Here was something much closer to the people than any recognized authority in England outside a few towns. This was the root of Scottish democracy: it may be said that the unprivileged Scot learned to be a citizen in the Church long before he could be an active citizen in the State.

In these conditions Scotland could not be governed, even after the Union, as England was governed. It had to be 'managed'. Personal influence over locally important people had, of course, a very important place in the government of Eighteenth-century England. In Scotland it was all. It could be exercised partly through the Scots members of the British Parliament. Scots representation at Westminster remained as feudal as it had been in Edinburgh before 1707. No doubt the Scottish Estates could, in fact, be influenced by public feeling and opinion as easily as most European parliaments of their day. In practice, contact between individual Scotsmen and members of the Estates was fairly easy when 154 lords and 161 commissioners of shires and burghs sat in Edinburgh. But in the British Parliament the Scots were reduced to sixteen peers and forty-five M.P.s. Sixty-one Scotsmen sitting in London were very far removed from the daily life of a nation the vast majority of whom had no share in choosing them. It is true that the rights represented in the Estates were carefully (too carefully) preserved under the Union Treaty. The whole body of Scots lords chose their sixteen representatives, who were (and are today) the only elected members of the House of Lords. To ensure that every royal burgh had its place in Parliament the towns were grouped, so that Glasgow, the second city in Scotland, had a quarter share in an M.P., like the village of New Galloway, with a population perhaps of 200.

Most of the electors of Scots M.P.s had very little interest in the politics of Westminster: the general body of Scotsmen had, of course, less interest still. British Ministers' main concern, so far as Scotland was concerned, was to secure as many of the Scottish votes in Parliament as possible: it was said that the Lord Advocate, usually the one Scottish Minister in the Commons, must always be a tall man so that Scots members might find it easy to follow him into the proper lobby. Successive 'managers' of Scots affairs worked hard to ensure that the right men (from the Government's point of view) were elected. Patronage flowed to the two or three thousand voters as well as to M.P.s themselves. These methods were usually successful: it was only when Government policy seemed to strike at some Scottish interest that M.P.s and peers were apt to draw together against it.

In a sense political Scotland was fossilized as it entered the Union. It was a fossil, however, with a certain life in it. On the whole Scotsmen were able to carry on most of their own affairs without violent change or interference. It was when the Union settlement was broken by the restoration of patronage in the appointment of parish ministers that the development of Scottish life was seriously disturbed. The Court of Session, itself, historically, a commission of the Scottish Parliament, had powers which allowed it to make what were really administrative decisions. When 'heritable jurisdictions'—the feudal courts and the rights of local magnates to act as sheriffs—were abolished after the last Jacobite rebellion, the practical autonomy of the countrysides suffered less than might have been expected; partly because the Church's part in local government was still extending, partly because the feudalizing spirit was still strong enough to hold its place in defiance of official policy. In 1773 Boswell and Johnson on their tour to the Hebrides found Highlanders performing services which looked feudal for a chief who had lost not only such legal powers as his ancestors may have had but also his land itself. Fifty years after the baronial courts were destroyed the Commissioners of Supply, who did some of the work of a modern county council, ceased to be nominated by Parliament, as they had been, and in future held office simply as owners of land paying tax on more than £200 a year: absolutely privileged and, in practice, irremovable.

A political change which, by modern standards, might have seemed serious, raised scarcely a ripple of protest. After the Union Scotland often had a Minister of her own in British Administrations, a Secretary of State nominally responsible for Scottish affairs. But the real 'managers' of Scotland were the second Duke of Argyll and his brother, the third Duke. After 1745 there were no more Scottish Secretaries for 140 years. In theory the country was supervised by the Secretary of State for the Northern Department, whose eye swept round Protestant Europe, but in fact Argyll's management continued till his death. A succeeding, and even more famous, managerial dynasty was that of the Dundases. Scarcely a vote was cast or the smallest Government appointment made in Scotland without the knowledge of Henry Dundas, first Viscount Melville (1742-1811). The system ended with the resignation of his son in 1827.

By this time the political spirit of Scotland had altered fundamentally. The early 'managers' had two aims—to make Scotland useful to the British Government and to ensure that the Government was useful to Scotland, or, at least, did not interfere awkwardly in what Scotsmen felt to be their own affairs. The first Argyll manager is said even to have hinted at rebellion when the Crown threatened to punish Edinburgh heavily for the Porteous Riot, in which its chief of police was publicly lynched. Corruptly, no doubt, but not without a hint of patriotism, the managers helped to keep the old national system of administration alive. They were aided by the growing tendency of governments to limit their own functions: in the days of Adam Smith *laissez-faire* was already in the air. But in the last quarter of the Eighteenth Century Scotsmen themselves began to look for change.

There is a sense in which the old, feudal Scotland died not with the Union or the abolition of heritable jurisdictions but with the American and French Revolutions and the growth of the first machine industries. There was a radical strain in Scottish political thinking at least as old as the Reformation. That eminently respectable judge, the father of James Boswell, praised Cromwell because 'he gart kings ken there was a lith in their neck' (*anglicè*, he made kings realize that there was a joint in their necks). In the Eighteenth Century there was a movement in some towns for popular election of their councillors. Perhaps it was the public commemoration by well-regarded Whig philosophers of the centenary of the Revolution of 1688 which really set the Scottish radical movement going. The French Revolution was only a year away. The Government in London, Dundas, its Scottish manager, and its agents in Scotland took alarm when they found themselves at war with revolutionary France. The law was stretched to allow a sweeping repression of men who considered themselves to be constitutional Reformers. In Scotland Radicalism was strongest among the weavers, who read and argued more than

other industrial workers. A strain of Scottish Nationalism soon found its way into their projects. Many of
those who stood most firmly for established ways
of government also felt that they were champions of
Scottish nationality. Sir Walter Scott wept when some
ancient sinecure offices were swept away: he felt that
the last relics of independent Scotland were going with
them.

The first Nineteenth-century reforms may have
seemed, in fact, to fit Scotland into a contemporary
English pattern. For the first time the middle-class Scot
who had no standing in the old world of feudalism and
privilege (beyond owning his house or garden, perhaps,
for which he was, and still is in Scots law, somebody's
vassal) was able to vote for an M.P. or a town councillor
like his English contemporary. For almost ninety years
after the Reform Bills of the 1830s the Whigs or Liberals
were usually in a majority in Scotland. When there was
a Liberal majority at Westminster, it sometimes rested
on Scots, Welsh and Irish M.P.s. This helped to give
Scotsmen a much more lively and general interest in
British politics than they had ever known before. In the
Eighteenth Century Scotland had produced only one
Prime Minister, the unpopular Earl of Bute, and one
leading figure in the House of Commons, Henry
Dundas. Between 1852 and 1935 there were six
Premiers of Scottish name and descent—Aberdeen,
Gladstone, Rosebery, Balfour, Campbell-Bannerman,
Bonar Law and Ramsay MacDonald. Though, out of
Scotland, some of these men may scarcely have seemed
to be Scots, it is not surprising that their countrymen

sometimes convinced themselves that their country was ruling the British Empire.

In the building of the Empire, Scotsmen took a large and distinguished part. Henry Dundas, who was, in effect, Minister for Indian and Scottish affairs at the same time, filled the East India Company's services with Scots, and Scotland continued to send administrators, merchants, soldiers and governors to the East after the Company gave place to the British-Indian Empire. Scottish emigration to the colonies was, proportionately, much heavier than English. Many of the great names in Canada's history are Scottish—the Mackenzies, explorer and reformer; Lord Selkirk, the organizer of the Red River Colony; Macdonald, the federalizer; Lord Strathcona, the railway builder; and a dozen more. Southern New Zealand was almost solidly Scots. Scottish missionaries have left a special mark in southern Africa. Two of the Australian capitals bear Scottish names: it was a Scot, Macarthur, who founded the Australian wool trade. In West and East Africa, too, many of the explorers, pioneers, and missionaries were Scots. During the Nineteenth Century, there was a continual movement between Scotland and the colonies. As late as the 1930s, all the Dominions and India had Scottish governors-general at the same time.

While Scotsmen thought themselves to be at the centre of a world-wide system, they were able to feel that their own country remained, in the main, their own affair. The Crown itself came back to Scotland. 'Balmorality', the revival of vaguely Jacobite Highland sentiment and a kilted social life while the Highlands were decaying, had its ironic side, but Queen Victoria's annual visits to her new castle in Aberdeenshire and her unmistakable pride in her Stewart ancestry did give Scotland, for the first time since the Union, a real link with the throne. This has developed so far that today Scotsmen are inclined simply to ignore anything that tends to separate them from the Royal Family, which seemed to draw still closer to them when the daughter of an ancient Scots house became Queen in 1936. In Scotland, Prince Philip is still the Duke of Edinburgh, the Prince of Wales was always Prince Charles,[1] when he was described officially as Duke of Cornwall, and the 'numeral' which links the Queen with Elizabeth Tudor is mentioned as seldom as possible. There were protests, sometimes violent, against the cypher 'EIIR' in 1952–3. Scotsmen are inclined to think it unnatural, since the first British Queen Elizabeth is descended not from the great Tudor, but from her victim, Mary Queen of Scots.

Nineteenth-century Scotland had its full share in the British Empire and in British Royalty. It even seemed to have a military existence. There were (and are) Lowland regiments which represent the old Scots Army of the Seventeenth Century, and kilted Highlanders first recruited among the clansmen in the Eighteenth. In the little wars of Queen Victoria's day, as in the great Napoleonic War before it, these were great names. Scots people were also able to feel that they had not lost

---

[1] His Scottish titles are Prince and Great Steward of Scotland, Duke of Rothesay, Earl of Carrick, Lord of the Isles and Baron of Renfrew.

control of what was most important in their own affairs. Party politics were interesting enough in their way, but economic affairs and the Church counted for much more. Victorian Governments interfered very little with industry and trade. Here almost everything was owned and managed in Scotland by Scots. Though the greatest ecclesiastical crisis of Victorian times, the Disruption of 1843, was in fact due to the refusal of British Governments to accept the Church of Scotland's demand that it should be freed from patronage, the struggle in the Kirk itself was far more absorbing than any political dispute, and it led to important changes in local government.

The Church was responsible for national education and for the care of the poor. When it split and the kirk session ceased to represent the majority of Protestants this state of things became unworkable. A new local body, the parochial board, was set up to deal with poor relief, and, later, with other parish business. It was partly elective. And to co-ordinate the work of the parochial boards a new sort of central authority was created. It was not a government department but a Board of Supervision, consisting of two lord provosts, three sheriffs, a law officer and three crown nominees. This change set the pattern for a whole system of local government and central administration—for elected school boards in each burgh and parish (1872), for county road trustees partly elected (1878) who opened the way for elected county councils (1889), for parish councils, wholly elected, which displaced the parochial boards (1894). Meanwhile new burghs were springing

up as 'populous places' were allowed to equip themselves with 'police powers' and councils to exercise
them. This practical and active local democracy may be
said to have grown out of and replaced the old social
work of the representative kirk sessions. At the centre
new independent boards and departments appeared—
the Scottish Board of Commissioners in Lunacy, the
Prison Commissioners, the Scottish Education Department, the Local Government Board for Scotland (which
replaced the Board of Supervision in 1894) and finally
the Scottish Board of Agriculture (to begin with mainly
concerned with Highland crofting) in 1911.

Thus a new framework of administration grew up in
Scotland. This can scarcely be said to have been planned
as a matter of general policy: as government entered
new fields of social life Scotland developed organs of her
own. Most of these were to some extent devolutionary—
they took over and enlarged functions that had been
carried out by government agencies for the whole of
Britain. The most important of all these devolutionary
steps was taken in 1885. Since the end of the 'Dundas
Despotism', the management of Scottish affairs had
been in the hands mainly of the Lord Advocate, the
chief Law Officer, though the Home Secretary was
responsible for them in the British Cabinet. National
feeling rebelled against the system, which became less
effective as the work of government increased. At last
a new Cabinet office, that of Secretary for Scotland, was
created: it did not become a secretaryship of state till
1926.

'Management' of one sort or another which had

allowed Scottish affairs to be given a special sort of treatment in an indirect or half-official way for nearly 180 years seemed now to be coming to an end, and Scotland to be emerging as a distinct unit in the organization of British Government. It looked for a time as if the movement must go further. Those were the days of the long Parliamentary struggles over Irish Home Rule. In the year after the first Secretary for Scotland was appointed a Scottish Home Rule Association was formed. It was already clear that the Secretary's influence in the British Cabinet was not likely to be very great. The idea that 'the Irish problem' might be solved by a system of Federal Home Rule, which would give an equal share of self-government to Scotland and Wales, was attractive to some English politicians. Liberal leaders, with the Scottish founder of the Labour party, Keir Hardie, and most of his followers, supported it. Between 1889 and 1913 the House of Commons discussed Bills or motions for Scottish Home Rule thirteen times: on eight of these there was a favourable vote. There was no powerful National Party: the Liberals filled this place, and enthusiasm for self-government was strongest among their young men and the Socialists. But the majority of Scottish M.P.s found it wise to accept the idea of autonomy, which seemed to be passing through that process under which projects are gradually found to be inevitable. In the end a spokesman of the Liberal Government declared that Home Rule for Scotland would follow the passing of the Bill for Irish Home Rule.

This was in the last days of peace before 1914. After

our years of world war the scene was changed. Scottish Home Rulers among M.P.s were still active: a Speaker's Conference even recommended a limited experiment in devolution for all the British countries. But the Liberal Party, which had been the most powerful voice of Scottish national feeling was wrecked. The loss of so many young Scotsmen, and economic depression coming after the strain and effort of war-time, had shaken the national self-confidence. What remained of political enthusiasm went mainly to the Labour Party, so many of whose first great names were Scots—Keir Hardie, Ramsay MacDonald, Arthur Henderson, and, among trade unionists, Robert Smillie. When, in 1922, Glasgow and the West of Scotland sent a majority of very vocal Labour members to Westminster, Scotsmen on the political Left could believe that their country was again about to lead Britain, perhaps the world—and to solve its own problems as it went, since all the Labourists were Home Rulers.

The Labour Party is still strong in Scotland: perhaps stronger than was indicated by the balance of Parliamentary seats in 1958, when the number of Scots Labourist M.P.s (35) just equalled that of the Conservatives (known, officially, as Unionists) and their allies, while Orkney and Shetland alone had a Liberal. But Scotland's part in the Labour movement has grown steadily less conspicuous as most of its trade unions merged with English ones and the first generation of the party's leaders disappeared. Mr. Tom Johnston is almost the last survivor of the days of its finest enthusiasm—a man who might conceivably have been British Prime

Minister if he had not preferred to immerse himself in
Scottish problems, attacked, no doubt, in the spirit of
practical Socialism but scarcely according to any rigid
party pattern.

As Socialist enthusiasm glowed and then dwindled
into accepted commonplace, self-conscious Nationalism
had been growing. Perhaps this was partly due, to begin
with, to the experience of young men who had found
themselves out of Scotland for the first time during the
war, and had learned with surprise that what they had
grown up to regard as normal British ways of life and
thought often belonged, in fact, to their country alone.
It was certainly fed by the long years of depression and
unemployment when Scottish industries were 'drifting
South'. It was sharpened, for some people, by the
arguments of Nationalism's Conservative opponents
who were apt to suggest that the Scots were a nation—
perhaps the only nation—who dared not attempt to pay
their own way or manage their own affairs. Its vehem-
ence was strengthened in 1929 when the system of local
government built up in the Nineteenth Century was
abruptly swept away.

The parish and the burgh were the cores of local
democracy in Scotland. Shire government had a feudal
tradition which clung to it even after the appearance of
elected county councils and, in a paradoxical way, showed
itself even now when some councillors are almost
professional politicians. The Local Government (Scotland) Act of 1929 destroyed the parish councils and
subordinated the smaller burghs to the county councils.
The countrysides of a land in which the small units of

local government had often been the most lively and active found themselves without free representative bodies whose members were in close touch with their neighbours. Burghs of over 20,000 people retained most of their old powers. The four cities had the rights, more or less, of English county burghs.

The main arguments for the change were financial: indeed there were no others which made any real impression on Scottish opinion. The Scottish Poor Law had never made any direct provision for able-bodied adults living in their own homes: though, in fact, relief of some kind had usually been found when it was desperately needed. In 1921, during the great post-war depression, the British Government suddenly found that thousands who had been kept alive by allowances under the Unemployment Insurance scheme had exhausted their claims on this fund. In England the Poor Law could support them, but not in Scotland. An Act which allowed parishes to maintain their unemployed was pushed hurriedly through Parliament. Scottish unemployment, however, was proportionately far heavier than English. Poor rates soared in the districts which were most depressed and least able to pay. When the Conservatives decided to de-rate industries and farming, and at the same time to recast Scottish local government, providing large grants to the new authorities, the Scottish councils were in no condition to resist.

No doubt the planners of this reform believed that the new system, fed by centralized grants, would be more easily managed from above, and this was true enough. They may also have thought that efficiency and economy would be found in larger units. Experience has scarcely supported that view. A distinctive and practically useful national tradition was lost: it has given way largely to a system of Welfare controlled from afar.

Developments at the centre of Scots affairs, on the other hand, have no doubt been in part a reply to Nationalist criticism. It is true that the series of bodies which have sought Home Rule have only once returned an independent Nationalist member to Parliament— Dr. Robert MacIntyre, who sat for a few months in 1945. But for more than a generation after 1920 support for the idea of self-government grew notably stronger, especially among Scottish writers and intellectuals, and there have been complicated and ingenious attempts to meet this feeling without the creation of a Scottish Parliament. Already in 1894 a House of Commons standing committee on Scottish Bills had been set up. This body, sometimes called the Scottish Grand Committee, consisted of all M.P.s from Scottish constituencies, with enough from other parts of the United Kingdoms to keep the great parties balanced as they are in the whole House. It might have served a very useful purpose. Scotsmen are apt to find that when important changes are to be made which affect their country—schemes of nationalization, or educational or legal reforms, for example—they are framed to suit English conditions in the first place; and that even where a separate Bill for Scotland is introduced the underlying policy does not seem to have been fully considered from a strictly Scottish point of view. Especially since

1948, when the Grand Committee was empowered to deal with the second reading of Bills that might be referred to it, there should have been an opportunity for Scots M.P.s to go somewhere near the root of this kind of difficulty. Perhaps, indeed, the Committee has sometimes corrected serious mistakes of Government planning. But it is seldom encouraged to deal with fundamentals and one cannot say that its proceedings are followed with any very intense interest in Scotland. As a sort of shadow parliament it has not proved to be very impressive even since it has debated the Scottish estimates for the year, while M.P.s have been apt to find that its meetings distracted them from other duties and interests. Its numbers have now been reduced. This change, which makes it less representative in a national sense, is intended to allow Scottish representatives to escape more easily from the burden of exclusively Scottish business.

Much more important was the development in administration which swept away the old Victorian central boards and grouped their officials into the four existing Departments under the Secretary of State. The change was made visible when almost all the civil servants who had worked in the Scottish Office in Whitehall were brought to Edinburgh and settled in the monumental block of St. Andrew's House, perched on the Calton Crag, which once carried a prison. This was 'administrative devolution' on a grand scale, from the general British point of view. Within Scotland it was administrative centralization. The framework of government was tighter than it had

ever been: control over local government was complete
and more direct.

Demands for self-government, or, at least, for
'legislative devolution'—a Parliament and Government
for Scottish affairs—did not die away when the administrators came North: indeed they grew louder and
stronger. No doubt the nationalization schemes of the
first Labour Government sharpened them. There were
hopes, at first, that the industries and services taken
over might be separately organized under independent
Scottish boards. But this did not happen. Scottish
'regional' headquarters and advisory councils were
certainly set up under most of the Acts of nationalization, but control was fixed in London. It is true that
since 1954 electricity, like gas, has been managed by
more or less autonomous Scottish bodies. In a sense this
brings things back to where they were before 1948, for
in Scotland these services had been owned and controlled largely by town councils: a Socialist Government
had, in fact, put an end to municipal Socialism, except
in transport, while other reforms reduced the local
councils' powers over poor relief and health services.

All these things combined to give vigour to a new
movement. Scottish Convention, an offshoot of the
Scottish National Party led by Mr. John MacCormick,
a Glasgow solicitor, called a National Assembly in 1948,
which decided to launch a new campaign for Home
Rule. The General Assembly of the Church of Scotland
had already hinted at legislative devolution. Next year
a second National Assembly launched the Scottish
Covenant, a document which was to be submitted for

signature to men and women throughout the country. The name and the idea were borrowed from the Covenants of the Seventeenth Century. This Covenant pledged its signatories to work 'in all loyalty to the Crown and within the framework of the United Kingdom' for 'a Parliament with adequate legislative authority in Scottish affairs'.

The response surprised the organizers of this movement: indeed it almost overwhelmed them. By 1951, they could claim to have received more than two million signatures—equivalent to considerably more than half the Scottish electorate. The great British political parties, however, made no response to this demonstration, and the Covenant Movement had been careful to insist that it was not itself a political party. It is probably true to say that the majority of adult Scots favoured some form of self-government, but opinion on the precise nature of the change that was most desirable had never crystallized effectively. The tentative 'Covenant plan' was for something like the Ulster Government and Parliament, but with greater control of finance. The National Party looked for Dominion Status. But powerful and strongly established groups of opinion, both Conservative and Labour, insisted that Scotland was too thoroughly integrated in the British economic system to be able to stand alone: under Home Rule, it was suggested, business might suffer and wages might fall. With fewer M.P.s at Westminster, Scotsmen, like Ulstermen, might have a smaller place in Imperial politics. The Covenant movement did not prove strong enough for its opportunity.

Some of its leaders involved themselves in an adventure of Glasgow University students, the removal of the Stone of Destiny from the Coronation Chair in Westminster Abbey. It must be said that Scots opinion as a whole showed a good deal of sympathy with what was sometimes called 'a vulgar theft'. The invader, Edward I of England, had carried off what he believed to be the Stone of Scone on which the ancient Scottish kings had sat at their inauguration. Scots had always felt it to be a national symbol and would have been glad to see it housed in Scotland between coronations. But in serious politics this was felt to be an irrelevancy. With the return of the Stone to Westminster, the Covenant Movement gradually lost force.

In 1952 the Conservative government appointed a Royal Commission on Scottish affairs whose terms of reference excluded any recommendation of self-government. The Balfour Commission heard evidence on the subject, however: its report proposed only minor changes in the existing system and seemed to stress the arguments it had heard against Home Rule. Most of its recommendations have been carried out. The Secretary of State now has his four subordinate ministers, and Edinburgh has an enlarged population of civil servants. Undoubtedly changes of this sort have created an important body of people who have a permanent interest in a Scottish administration and know many of its problems well. But a certain political unease remains. It cannot be said that many Scottish Ministers, even Secretaries of State, have taken a very high place in British politics in our day: essentially they are still managers of a country with an obstinately individual life of its own which is apt to fret against the increasingly rigid framework of modern government from a distance, though the machinery of management is now more formal, more closely integrated than it has ever been and some of the bodies it has to deal with are less effectively autonomous because the financial independence of local councils (for instance) has been lost. Devolution which is merely administrative begins to look more and more anomalous as the years go by.

Chapter Eight

ARTS AND VOICES

LIKE some other small European peoples which began to build up their national identity about the time when Scotland successfully asserted its own nationhood in the Wars of Independence, the Scots have always shared one language or more with their neighbours. There are two main differences, however, between the Scottish situation and that of Switzerland or Belgium. One of the languages which Scotland has shared, Gaelic, is now spoken by very few, and there was, for a time, a Scots literary language as distinct as (say) Czech or Portuguese, which still lives in speech and poetry and has influenced the thought and expression even of Scottish people who seldom try to use it.

Gaelic was the language which the first Scots colonists brought from Ireland. Till the Twelfth Century it was the language of government in most parts of Scotland. Since then it has been retreating, at times slowly, now very fast indeed. Its strength in the Middle Ages and earlier was the link with Gaelic Ireland, less than twenty sea-miles from Kintyre, Galloway and the nearest of the Hebrides. This link, first partly broken by the Viking invasions, was cut much more completely at the beginning of the Seventeenth Century, when the Plantation of Ulster interposed a body of colonists, mainly Lowland Scots, between Gaelic Ireland and the

Gaelic Highlands. By this time most Scottish Gaels were becoming Protestant. Gaelic remained the language of Irish Roman Catholics, and this religious breach has done more to separate the two peoples and weaken the old language permanently than the physical existence of the English-speaking, Protestant Six Counties.

For centuries the Scots and Irish Gaels had shared the same poetry and legend, the same bardic traditions. Scots Gaelic poetry took new rhythms and colour in the work of Mary Macleod (Mairi nighean Alasdair Ruadh), Ian Lom (MacDonald), Alasdair macMhaister Alasdair (Alexander MacDonald), Rob Donn (Mackay), Duncan Ban (Macintyre). This group of Seventeenth- and Eighteenth-century verse-makers, freer and less professional than the old bards, are its greatest names. It sank during the Nineteenth Century, however. In our own day at least two notable Gaelic poets have appeared and real efforts have been made to revive (or at least preserve) the language and traditional music that went with it by bodies like An Commun Gaidhealach (the Gaelic Association) and by ministers of the Protestant churches, which were once hostile to it; but the will for a Gaelic revival has not been strong enough to bridge the national and religious gulf between Scottish and Irish Gaeldom. Even among the enthusiasts of Scottish Nationalism there has been very little support for the idea that Gaelic should be imposed as a national language on Scots people, most of whom have known nothing of it for centuries. Irish experience certainly cannot encourage any plan of that sort.

Traditional Gaelic song and story are now being collected systematically by the Edinburgh University School of Scottish Studies, which has taken up this work from the Scandinavian and Irish folk-lorists and the individual collectors who first organized it. But, at present, it seems doubtful whether Scots Gaelic, as a living speech, will survive our century unless the North-West and the Isles find new vigour to support it.

Scotland's other shared language has been English—more or less. In its beginnings the speech of the Anglic Lowlands was scarcely distinguishable from that of Northern England. The poem which sounds the first clear note of fully conscious nationalism in Scotland, perhaps in Europe, Barbour's *Brus* (1375), an epic (or rhymed biography) of the hero-king of the Wars of Independence, would perhaps have been almost as easily understood in York as in Aberdeen. A century later, however, Scotland had a literary language which was unmistakably her own: the language of poets, of the court, and the law. After decades of war, Scotsmen ceased to borrow from England: this was as true of speech as of other things. Meanwhile a standard literary English had established itself which belonged to the Midlands or London, and was very far from the language of Scotsmen. The extraordinary group of *makaris* who produced an unequalled body of Scots poetry just before or after the year 1500—Robert Henryson, William Dunbar and Gavin Douglas—were all admirers of Chaucer, but, in words and syntax as well as in spirit, their work is very different from his. It belongs unmistakably to another tongue which was

taking what it needed for itself from Latin and French.
To a Scot at least each of these very individual poets
seems to begin where Chaucer left off. Henryson has
stateliness and moral solidity as well as a remarkably
sympathetic humour. Dunbar has an inexhaustible
command of metres, moods and colour. Gavin Douglas
is a scholar and theorist of letters, a painter of scenes
and seasons.

Scots prose of that time, what remains of it, is equally
distinct. Its development was broken by the Reformation. It may have been partly because he wished to be
read in England that John Knox wrote a language which
is scarcely Scots—in the short extracts from the first
Buke of Discipline printed in Chapter IV of the present
book the spelling alone has been modernized: yet they
contain scarcely a word whose use may seem strange to
English readers. What was decisive for the future of
Scots prose, however, was the Reformers' acceptance of
the English translation of the Bible. Henceforth this was
the book best-known to Scots people of all classes. Its
language gradually became the correct one for most
sorts of serious writing.

The decline of literary Scots may have been hastened
a little by the fact that in the Sixteenth Century and the
beginning of the Seventeenth the Scottish writers whose
names meant most to the great world of letters were
using Latin. This was, of course, the language of medieval philosophers and chroniclers in Scotland, as
elsewhere in Europe, but the great age of Scots Latinists
came only with the Renaissance. George Buchanan
(1500–82) had a wider international reputation than any

Scottish writer before the age of David Hume and Walter Scott—for his poems and plays rather than for his History of Scotland, the elaborate falsehoods of his attack on his patroness, Mary Queen of Scots, or his pamphlet *De Jure Regni apud Scotos*, which had considerable influence on political thought. Arthur Johnston (1587–1641) was almost as highly regarded as a poet. He wrote charmingly and naturally about his own Aberdeenshire countryside. By his time the stream of Scots verse had been abruptly checked by another influence, a royal one, when James VI of Scotland went to London as James I.

The Stewart kings were a writing race, but none as persistently and ambitiously so as this James, who would have surely been a rather pedantic, though respected, man of letters if he had not been born to the throne. The poets of the Sixteenth Century still wrote Scots, and James, who would have liked to be their leader, produced the first work of criticism in the language, his *Reulis and Cautelis to be Observit and Eschewit in Scottis Poesie* (1585). Once he was King of England, however, James wished to belong to English literature, and the Scots poets whom he influenced began, quite abruptly, to write in English too. The speech of the country did not change: indeed a very little study of the stately verse of William Drummond (1585–1649) will show that what was spelled as English was pronounced as Scots. Ballads which are among the chief glories of Scottish poetry were still being composed and sung. But, as a written language, Scots had begun to disappear well over half a century before the Union of 1707.

Half a century later it was alive again. This rebirth is very remarkable. It might never have happened but for one man, a lively poet of real, though rather limited, talent, Allan Ramsay, who died in 1758. Ramsay was a patriotic Scot who looked on the Union as a catastrophe. He was an enterprising bookseller and publisher in Edinburgh as well as a writer of songs, mock elegies and a pastoral comedy, *The Gentle Shepherd*. He seems to have set out quite deliberately to revive writing in Scots. In his *Tea Table Miscellany* he published traditional songs, often re-written to suit contemporary taste. In *The Evergreen* he offered the Eighteenth Century some of the poems of the *makaris*, also suitably modified. Scots people were overjoyed to find their own speech in print.[1] Ramsay's songs, original or revived, and his *Gentle Shepherd* were enormously popular. He set a pattern of poetic writing that was followed by polite gentlewomen and town wits; above all by two men of genius far beyond his own, Robert Fergusson (1750–74) and Robert Burns (1759–96).

Scotland was now emerging into a new age of letters, what is called Edinburgh's Golden Age. The capital, deserted by kings and rulers, burst into a blaze of genius, as fully recognized abroad as at home. This renaissance did not belong to one city alone: it was a national thing. It is true that some of its most famous men and their works now look a little dim. David Hume's philosophy and Adam Smith's economics will always be read, but William Robertson's histories, the rhetoric of

[1] James Watson had published a first collection of poems mainly in Scots in 1706.

Hugh Blair, *The Grave* of Robert Blair, the drama of John Home are never likely to make much stir in the world again. James Macpherson's *Ossian*, a curious paraphrase of Gaelic legend which, like so much in Scottish literature before the modern revival, echoed regret for the defeat of the last Jacobite rising in 1746, carried a romantic view of Scotland round the world. The leaders of the Golden Age were self-consciously cosmopolitan and enlightened, though usually with a Presbyterian background very different from that of the Continental Enlightenment. All of them wrote in English and some were at great pains to learn to speak it correctly too. But it is precisely what is most Scots in this literary revival, Burns's poems and Sir Walter Scott's novels (which came at the end of it), that has lasted best.

In the minds (and hearts) of Scots people Robert Burns is a unique figure. He is a national hero: perhaps there is no other European poet whose name is so cherished by his countrymen. St. Andrew's Day is the patriotic feast of Scots abroad, but at home Burns Nicht (25th January, the poet's birthday) is a far better-recognized occasion for public suppers and speech-making. Undoubtedly some who attend these gatherings seldom read a verse of Burns's poetry (or of any other) and would scarcely understand it if they did, now that many of them are losing their command of the Scots vocabulary. For them he is a symbol, a type of the nation: a lover of liberty, democratic ('the ploughman poet'), humorous, sentimental, intensely human ('all too human', say reverend orators, indulgently but not unjustly), poor and independent-minded, above all, completely Scottish.

Certainly it is not altogether for these reasons, which have little to do with poetry or letters, that 'the Immortal Memory of Robert Burns' stands so astonishingly high. The Scots have been a reading, singing people, and by any standard Burns is a very remarkable poet indeed. He has puzzled generations of academic writers, who used to label him 'romantic', though he belongs so clearly to the social, realistic Eighteenth-century world. He has embarrassed teachers even in Scotland who have been anxious to fit him into a frame of English literature which will not hold him. Burns did, indeed, belong to a school of poetry which he consciously developed and tried to preserve, the school of popular song-writing and social comment in Scots. His 'message' was the rebelliously kindly one (coloured by the optimism of the age of Enlightenment which rejected Predestination) summed up in a famous and much debated verse, the expression of his hope that even the Devil may escape damnation:

> But, fare you weel, auld Nickie-ben!
> O wad ye tak a thought an men!
> Ye aiblins might—I dinna ken—
>   Still hae a *stake*—
> I'm wae to think upo' yon den
>   Ev'n for your sake![1]

---

[1] *Aiblins* is perhaps, *stake* a claim to salvation, *wae* sad. It is typical of Burns and many of the Scots Eighteenth-century poets that the spelling of many words is English though the readers were expected to give them a Scots pronunciation: 'thought', for instance, would be *thocht*.

Technically, Burns was a master of ringing verse, of conciseness, of evocative phrases, of laughter, derision and tenderness: but though he thought much and deeply about his art he seldom wrote anything which his own farming folk would find it hard to follow. It is, perhaps, chiefly because he used words superbly to speak to simple people that he has remained the one great literary figure whom a whole country can idolize. With him, poetry in the Scots tongue reached a culmination: for more than a century all who wrote verse in the language (a dwindling band, first in quality, then in numbers) followed the tradition that he sanctified. In a sense his immense popularity is the culmination of another side of Scots writing. In most countries authors and poets have expected to be read by a restricted class of educated people. No doubt this was true of early Scots poets, some of whom certainly wrote for the court, but from the end of the Seventeenth Century till our own day most Scottish writers of quality, whether they used Scots or English, have aimed at the widest possible audience. In a small country where most people had a little book-learning this was, perhaps, natural enough. At the same time, poetry lived as much in ballads and remembered lays as in books. These things have meant that for Scots there has never been quite the same sharp division between sophisticated writing and folk-literature that has been common elsewhere. A folk-literature of a kind, transmitted as much by ear as by eye, still persists after a century and a half of industrialization. It produces new songs, even ballads, in Scots (perhaps none of them very remarkable poetically) and some of Burns's own songs belong to it—they are known, though imperfectly, to thousands who have never read them carefully.

Walter Scott, who came next to Burns in fame and popularity in his own country, and was far more influential elsewhere, also has his links with this folk-culture. The best of his prose—his dialogue, and such things as 'Wandering Willie's Tale'—is Scottish in idiom. Only his stories of Scotland are truly alive now, though books like *Ivanhoe* and *Kenilworth* were read everywhere in their day, and for generations after. Strong commonsense, a hearty and penetrating interest in human character, and a feeling for tragedy that is sustained by his own regrets for the vanishing life of a heroic, independent, uncommercial Scotland gave their peculiar quality to such novels as *The Heart of Mid-lothian*, *Old Mortality* and *Redgauntlet*. The strain of poetry in Scott's thought and feeling expressed itself better in novels (and songs) than in his verse romances, enormously popular as they were, readable as they are still. His feeling for romance, indeed, is one of his less important qualities, though he set a style of romantic novel-writing for Europe and America. No doubt there is a sense in which nearly all Scottish art is romantic— the strictly limited sense, however, that it leaves those who enjoy it something to dream about.

It is not by accident that this greatest and most formative of Scottish novelists wrote mainly about the past. It was in its past that Scotland lived for him: no writer has ever understood the atmosphere, the form and flavour of post-medieval Scotland as he did. Beyond this, however, there is a sense in which almost all novels by Scotsmen are stories about history. Among Scottish writers the feeling for time seems to be particularly strong. They are scarcely able to think of the present as something without beginning or end. Even if they are dealing (as Scott himself sometimes did) with events that may be supposed to have happened only ten or twenty years before, they seem driven to make a picture of a period which is over. The ablest of Scott's rivals, John Galt (1779–1839), who wrote in a prose which was often scarcely English in anything but spelling, has left in *Annals of the Parish* a matchless description of the effects on the Ayrshire countryside of the first stages of the Industrial Revolution, which were taking place when he was a boy. Galt was a truly original story-teller, as James Hogg (1770–1835) was in his extraordinarily vivid and powerful study of demonic possession, the *Memoirs and Confessions of a Justified Sinner*, whose setting is a hundred years before his day. It was the Scott tradition which dominated novel writing in the Nineteenth Century almost as completely as Burns's did the writing of verse in Scots. Robert Louis Stevenson (1850–94), the most accomplished of Scottish Victorian novelists, belongs to both: his graceful Scots poetry is Burns for the drawing-room.

By Stevenson's time, however, the Golden Age was no more than a memory. The most successful Scottish writers no longer wrote in Scotland. No doubt it was ill-health that drove Stevenson himself into exile. Perhaps the South Seas could not have held him if he had not found in them a sort of tropical reflection of ancient Hebridean life and legend. But literature had already moved to London. Expatriate Scots had lived and written there since the days of James Thomson (1700–48) and Tobias Smollett (1721–71) or earlier. Now serious writing in Scotland almost died away. Even the *Edinburgh Review*, which had been the very influential voice of clever young Scots under the Regency, had gone south in 1847. The most enduring books published in Edinburgh in those years were reminiscences—Hugh Miller's *My Schools and Schoolmasters* (1852) and Lord Cockburn's posthumous *Memorials* (1856) and *Journal* (1874). Nineteenth-century Scotland remained a highly individual, indeed a highly successful country in many ways, but, except for its newspapers—the only ones seen by most Scotsmen—it had nothing to offer in letters but weakening echoes of the past and the rural sentimentalities of the 'Kailyaird School'. To write profitably about his country a Scotsman had to present it in a way that London publishers and their readers would understand and enjoy. In the work of a succession of expatriates, from Thomas Carlyle (1795–1881), to Sir James Barrie (1860–1937), a playwright of enormous skill, and the crown of the Kailyaird, Scots readers learned to see themselves as a sort of second-hand reflection in other people's mirrors.

While literary art declined in Victorian Scotland, other arts were livelier. The Nineteenth Century was an age of painters. The oldest representational art of historic times in Scotland is the lively and beautiful work of Pictish stone carvers and of the Gaels and

Lowland church decorators who followed them in the Middle Ages. A continuous tradition of easel painting scarcely reaches back beyond the Seventeenth Century. Its first great names belong to Eighteenth-century portrait painters: Allan Ramsay (1713–84), son of the poet, was the chief of these. The men and women of the Golden Age are recorded with a Burnsian gusto and skilful simplicity by Sir Henry Raeburn (1756–1823). The first notable landscape and subject painters belong to the same period, among them Sir David Wilkie (1785–1841), John Thomson (1778–1840) and David Scott (1806–49). Edinburgh became consciously a centre of pictorial art. The Royal Scottish Academy, founded in 1826, has remained, on the whole, remarkably representative for such a body. Scottish art showed considerable independence. William McTaggart (1835–1910) was painting impressionistically before the French Impressionists. The Glasgow School, whose leading spirit was W. Y. Macgregor (1855–1903), borrowed from France and Japan, but their absorbing interest in colour and the quality of light, very natural in men who passed their lives in the West of Scotland, gave them an individuality which Europe found impressive. There is a peculiar quality of *fin de siècle* romance in the otherwise sturdy portraits of Sir James Guthrie, the landscapes of George Henry and E. A. Walton, even the etchings of Sir D. Y. Cameron and Sir Muirhead Bone and the wit of Joseph Crawhall.

Architecture has been the queen of the visual arts for Scotsmen. Most of the great medieval Scottish churches are ruins now, but one can get an idea of their quality from Glasgow Cathedral, the granite of St. Machar's, Aberdeen, and Iona Abbey—where conventual buildings have been reconstructed, with understanding skill, by the Iona Community under the guidance of Ian Lindsay. There is a certain starkness in this Scottish gothic, which, towards the end of the Middle Ages, was apt either to return to the bare solidity of its beginnings or occasionally to break into exuberant decoration, which, in the fantastic stone-carving of Roslin Chapel, near Edinburgh, becomes almost Portuguese or Indian. The high, rectangular towers which, after the War of Independence, were Scotland's characteristic fortresses and the homes of its nobles, also flowered into fantasy as the Middle Ages ended. The tall, bare walls were crowned with corbelled turrets and high-reaching crow-stepped gables. One can see the change from this last gothic extravagance to the baroque [1] in George Heriot's Hospital, Edinburgh. A more modest and very widespread form of the baroque is known as the Scottish Vernacular, throwing its gables towards the sky in the high 'lands' of Edinburgh, breaking its roof-lines with carved dormer windows in smaller buildings.

In the work of Sir William Bruce (died 1710) who had himself been concerned with the completion of Heriot's long after the death of its first builder, William Wallace, in 1631, this style gave way to classicism. He was the forerunner of a remarkable succession of Scots architects, many of whom worked chiefly in England.

---

[1] Or Renaissance: but Italy is far from Scotland. There is a glimpse of the true Renaissance in the lovely palace at Stirling, which has long been a barracks.

William Adam (died 1748) and his sons, most notably the brilliant Robert (1728–92), were builders of country palaces, town streets and public institutions. The classical tradition struck deep roots in Scotland when, in the last quarter of the Eighteenth Century, Edinburgh broke out of its medieval bounds and set up a New Town of monumental terraces and squares. Robert Adam's Charlotte Square is, no doubt, the finest thing of its kind, but the general pattern of classical town building in stone maintained itself in some form through most of the Nineteenth Century. Most of western and southern Edinburgh and Victorian Glasgow belong to it. Oddly enough, though the idea of Gothic Revival came partly from Sir Walter Scott, it did not make much of a mark on Scots towns except in church, university (and occasionally municipal) buildings. In what were called 'Scottish Baronial' castles and villas it produced some extraordinary huddles of stone. But the most distinguished Victorian architects, from W. H. Playfair (1789–1857) to Alexander ('Greek') Thomson (1817–1875) and Sir John J. Burnett (1857–1938), followed classical or Renaissance styles in the main, though some of them were ready to turn their hands to anything. From the days of the Adams onwards Scottish towns were almost completely rebuilt and the mark of the classical school is strong on most of them. Taste declined as Victorian opulence advanced. The feeling for proportion in building weakened. Windows bulged and there was a good deal of vulgar ostentation in stone. Fashion among critics of architecture (such as they were) disowned the classical tradition, but it lingered in the half-conscious preference of Scots people, backed by a remarkable inheritance of skill among masons and other craftsmen, who knew how to handle its themes. When, as the Victorian Age ended, the minds of designers turned towards older Scottish styles, Charles Rennie Mackintosh (1868–1928) produced buildings at once startlingly 'modern' and functional and intensely traditional. His Glasgow School of Art, which had no parallel in Britain (and very few elsewhere) long after its completion in 1907, has the lines as well as the simplicity of the best of the old castles before their builders had learnt extravagance. His houses are 'Vernacular' for the Twentieth Century—the proper models, one would have imagined, for the years to come when towns set about surrounding themselves with 'schemes' of simply built municipal cottages.

It seemed half a century ago that Scotland had found an architecture capable of using new materials in a way that was her own; just as it seemed that Scottish litera-ture was quietly dying with the last successors of Burns and Scott; that with a group of post-impressionists, S. J. Peploe, F. C. B. Cadell, Leslie Hunter and J. D. Fergusson, Scottish painting could develop pleasantly and colourfully from the point where the Glasgow School had left it; that, on the economic side of things, Scottish business would continue to control its own prosperous development; that, in politics, Scottish Liberalism was firmly set and was moving gently towards some sort of self-government. All these expec-tations were falsified after the 1914–18 War. By that time C. R. Mackintosh had gone into exile: it was twenty years or more before new buildings at all comparable with his were seen again in Scotland when Robert Hurd, among others, began to revive the Scottish architectural idiom. Painting has no doubt been struggling towards a new style: the break with the old has been less shattering here than in some other countries, but W. G. Gillies is one of the few names of real distinction in either. No doubt the fearful economic depression of the 'Twenties and 'Thirties threw a shadow over these arts, as over education and the easy development of politics. And yet it was precisely in the years of change and unemployment that a new literary life and a new strengthening of national consciousness were born.

The Scottish Renaissance as a literary movement was launched at the end of the Kaiser's War by Christopher Murray Grieve, then a journalist, and both then and since a very remarkable poet, writing under the name of Hugh MacDiarmid. Whether anything of the kind could or would have existed without the powerful thrust of this sometimes erratic dynamo it is hard to say. Literary talent and patriotic feeling were clearly waiting to be attracted by the idea of Scotland as a country with an active and lively culture of its own and a future equal to its past. The most important of modern Scots novelists, Neil M. Gunn, and the most sensitive of Scots critics, who has also been the most impressive of recent Scots poets writing in English, Edwin Muir (1887-1959), were quickly attracted by the movement though Muir left it later. A whole series of poets and novelists have followed, some of them disciples of

Mr. Grieve's, some of them merely drawn by a new opportunity to write about the country and live in it. The flow of Scottish literary talent towards London, which had been consistent for generations, was checked. Some who were established there returned to write at home. Today there is, in the country, something that had not been seen for more than a century, a body of writers deeply interested in Scotland, not merely as a picturesque or comic background, but as something very important to themselves and the future.

One can scarcely say, as yet, how far this rebirth of Scottish letters or the work it has produced are likely to last. It aimed, to begin with, both at putting new meaning and a revived national feeling into Scottish writing and at the revival of Scots as a literary tongue. Hugh MacDiarmid's most important poems, including the extraordinary *A Drunk Man Looks at the Thistle*, in which he surveys his country, himself, and the world, are in Scots of one kind or another. William Soutar (1898–1943) used the language with even greater technical mastery, and a succession of younger and still surviving poets have written in it. But for most of these men and women it is not, and probably never has been, the speech of everyday life, and almost all of them have written English verse too.

Scots dialect is still very widely spoken, particularly in country places. It is still more widely understood: this can be seen in the theatre when a good play in Scots is put on. Probably it is true that many who seldom use more than an occasional Scots phrase in speaking tend to fall into the old language when they try to write verse, just as audiences expect Scots songs in a pantomime. But the poets of the Scottish Renaissance have not succeeded in making songs or even satire for the people, as those of the Eighteenth Century did. Perhaps, like other Twentieth-century poets, they have been too much concerned with themselves, their own perplexities and illuminations. For the first time since the Middle Ages, some of the leading figures in Scottish letters have been writing for an élite, a consciously 'literary' public. No doubt that is the price that has to be paid by those who, like Hugh MacDiarmid, aim at putting new ideas into verse. When hopes of a rebirth of the language are concerned it may be a heavy price. Much more than the rather naive condemnation of 'Plastic Scots' (or 'Lallans') because it is apt to break with the consecrated dialect of Burns and Fergusson, it has limited the effect of this side of the Renaissance movement.

Prose writing has looked towards a wider public, in Scotland and elsewhere. Attempts to revive Scots for this purpose have not made much headway, though Lewis Grassic Gibbon (J. Leslie Mitchell, 1901–35) used a rhythmic prose that is Scots in idiom in his passionate *Scots Quair*. This trilogy of novels records the life of North-East Scotland in the first thirty years of the century with a remarkable sense of period and from the point of view of a sort of National Marxism which he shared with Hugh MacDiarmid. Neil M. Gunn is the first Highland novelist to have written with real distinction about the contemporary life of his own people. Unlike his literary forefather among picaresque novelists, Smollett, Eric Linklater has kept a home and a persistent background in Scotland. Agnes Mure Mackenzie (1891–1955) provided Scotsmen with a gracefully written reinterpretation of their past from a point of view at once nationalist and royalist. George Scott-Moncrieff has described the country itself with loving perception. Many others, nearly all influenced in some degree by the sense of national revival, have written and are writing as poets, story-tellers, historians, critics.

Yet the material, the purely economic basis of this new literature remains curiously, indeed dangerously, narrow. It is remarkable enough that we should have seen in the last thirty years this flood of Scottish writing, without any great revival of publishing in Scotland, though one or two Scottish publishers have been doing distinguished work. Mr. Grieve himself has been responsible for a series of little reviews, none of them very long-lasting. There have been other magazines—*Outlook*, *The New Alliance*, *The Scots Review*, and now *The Saltire Review*—all dealing with Scottish problems intelligently and printing new work, but most books about Scotland still come from London.

The spoken word now supplements (or supplants) the written one, but the story of radio in Scotland is oddly anomalous. When regular broadcasting began in 1922, Scottish self-confidence was at its lowest ebb. It is impossible to believe that, at any other time, a people who had long had most other cultural media in their own hands—Church, schools, newspapers—would have accepted a monopoly in a new form of communication over which Scotsmen had no sort of control, except in the sense that its executive head, now Lord Reith, was a Scot. The weight of reviving national sentiment has certainly induced the B.B.C. to give a Scottish colour to its regional Home Service and finally to accept a Scottish Broadcasting Council, formally in charge of the service for Scotland. Undoubtedly this has helped to provide a living and an occasional platform for a number of Scottish writers, besides giving Scots people, and particularly Gaelic-speakers, a chance of hearing something about themselves and their country. The Scottish Renaissance has its radio echoes. But because the basis of the B.B.C. programmes and their approach to the world's affairs is not Scottish those items that are designed for Scotland are apt (in spite of the best intentions) to have a provincial air. The Scottish Broadcasting Council does not control B.B.C. Television. Scottish Television Limited provides a rival independent service.

Radio has given some useful support to one of the most important things in the literary revival. For the first time, since the Reformation at least, Scotland has something like a recognizable national drama. For three centuries or more the Reformed Kirk frowned on the theatre, but in this century the atmosphere has changed. The immense success of Sir James Barrie as a playwright, chiefly for London, the example of Ireland, which inspired the founders of the enterprising Glasgow Repertory Theatre in 1912 and the Scottish National Theatre Company which followed it, and then the sudden sweeping development of the Community Drama Movement in the 1920s all helped to make it possible for Scots dramatists to hope to see their plays performed at home. Some were at work even before 1914, but the real star of this new illumination did not rise till more than a dozen years after that. He was James Bridie (O. H. Mavor, 1888-1951) who combined the fantasy, a good deal of the stagecraft, and a little of the sentiment of Barrie with some of the wit of Bernard Shaw and an odd, defensive devil-worship of his own. Bridie, who was very much a Glasgow product to begin with, gradually linked himself with the Scottish Renaissance. Some of his plays, *The Anatomist* and *A Sleeping Clergyman*, for instance, were international successes, but such a thing as *The Forrigan Reel* is so Scottish as scarcely to be intelligible elsewhere. In his light, and largely as a result of his personal effort, professional theatres which devote themselves largely to new Scots drama were organized first in Glasgow, then in Edinburgh. Some of the new playwrights write successfully in Scots, most notably Robert McLellan, whose *Jamie the Saxt* is a brilliant historical comedy. As yet there is no real successor to Bridie, but there are many dramatists and the new Scottish theatre does seem to have life in it.

What is most distinctively Scottish in music still belongs, perhaps, to the world of folk-art. Long years of training have always been needed to make a good bagpipe player. The pipes have become, through centuries, the traditional instrument of the Gael, and in our day the Celtic harp (clarsach) has been revived, largely to accompany singing. Great skill and knowledge go to the composition of pibrochs and of new dance tunes for the violin. But though Scotland now has two full-scale professional orchestras and other well-established means of music-making, art-music of a conventional kind is still struggling to find a native quality.

Scottish country dancing, on the other hand, is a folk art which has leapt into new life in the past generation. This is not the revival of a dead tradition. Country dancing survived in Scotland when it had disappeared elsewhere, but it was a dwindling thing when a revival was deliberately planned by Miss Jean Milligan and Mrs. Stewart of Fasnacloich in 1923. Today it is practised everywhere in Scotland and by thousands in other countries who are not Scots. It is carefully (some think almost too carefully) supervised by the Royal Scottish Country Dance Society. Half-forgotten niceties have been re-established. Old dances, old tunes have been rediscovered and new ones struggle for recognition. These lively and triumphant airs set hearts as well as feet stirring. People of all classes and almost all ages give themselves to the reel and strathspey with attentive vigour and unmistakable enjoyment. The movement has some unexpected aspects: in North-Eastern Ireland (one is told) Scottish country dancing is an expression of Protestant loyalty, in contrast with Irish dancing, which is Roman Catholic and Republican. In Scotland, however, this is one form of national revival which has no political flavour. Here, at least, the sort of Scotsman whose attitude to himself and his country has been formed by long memories of 'Scoatch' jokes in music-hall has learned not to be ashamed of being Scottish.

Sport too has a voice, sometimes a very strident one. Football is the national sport of modern Scotland—for the great majority of Scots association football played by professionals, rugby football for middle-class amateurs. Scotsmen took a great part in the development of both games. They are ruled in Scotland by national bodies, powerful and, at times, powerfully criticized. Golf is almost a Scots creation: its international headquarters have been at St. Andrews. Shinty, something like a fiercer form of hockey, is the Highland game. But the greatest moments in the sporting year are the days of international football matches, especially those with England. These are the occasions when, for many Scots people, their country comes to life most fully—in recent years sometimes disappointingly.

This record of dancing, drama, letters and eager play makes a bright picture—perhaps too bright. It suggests a people full of national vigour, both physical and mental, who are learning after (and through) a long depression to be lively again: but that is scarcely what Scots people think of themselves, or perhaps what strangers see in Scotland. It is true that a number of bodies have established themselves in the last forty years (besides the political and economic ones) which are working, as no one did before, to conserve or expand something from the Scottish past—the Country Dance Society, just mentioned, the National Trust for Scotland, which has saved interesting buildings from destruction, the Association for the Preservation of Rural Scotland, the Saltire Society (taking its name from the national flag of St. Andrew) which has helped to restore a sense of style to municipal building through its housing awards, has republished Scots classics, organized Scots singing and recitation, issued reports on radio and schools, and has had a hand in launching the youngest of these organizations, aimed at the development of inherited taste, the Scottish Craft Centre. In the last few years the Scottish Committee of the Arts Council and the Historic Buildings Council for Scotland have been able to give official support to some cultural work of this sort.

But there is another side to this picture. Probably most Scots people are only rather vaguely aware of such activities. They are not unfriendly to them, but their education has not prepared Scotsmen to understand them fully. The newspapers that circulate most widely in Scotland are no longer owned there. Editions of London papers printed in Glasgow or Edinburgh have added the word 'Scottish' to their titles, but though it is still true that Scotland has more individual newspapers, for the size of its population, than any other part of Great Britain (among them two of a notably solid and informative kind, *The Glasgow Herald* and *The Scotsman*) the average reader no longer sees the world through the eyes of Scottish journalists only. The view of himself that the press and radio give him has an increasingly provincial tinge.

Educated Scotsmen are certainly more apt to be conscious of their nationality than they were when the rest of the world seemed remoter than it is now, and this is probably true of the less educated too, though the subconscious sense of nationality has always been very strong in them, and is not, perhaps, seriously shaken by American influences which are sometimes quite as prevailing as English ones. Scotsmen still speak with a voice of their own, even in the most literal sense. Their English knows nothing of the intrusive 'r' or the dropping of the 'h' that goes with a 'w'. Indeed, but for broadcasting the very rapid changes our time has seen in the pronunciation of southern English might have made it almost unintelligible to them. But, in some ways, they are less certain of themselves than they used to be. It is not untypical that, in the series of International Festivals of Music and the Arts which Edinburgh has organized since the war, the quality of correct internationalism has been held to exclude most of what is Scottish: except for Robert Kemp's striking version of the Sixteenth-century *Satyre of the Thrie Estaits* by David Lyndsay at the first Festivals, nothing Scottish in music, drama or painting has come near to dominating Edinburgh's autumn, and nothing has been expected or encouraged to do so by the Scotsmen who control these often brilliant displays of varied virtuosity.

EPILOGUE

SCOTLAND, it was argued in the first pages of this book, is a very unusual thing by Twentieth-century standards: a country which is, at least in some sense, a nation, but in no sense a State. This is, I hope, borne out by what has been said about the various sides of its life. Can anything so anomalous continue to exist in this modern world? No doubt the earth and rock that are the physical framework of Scotland will not disappear, but Scotland as a human entity could vanish—and not only in the sense that all nations may be destroyed if mankind, in this century, commits nuclear suicide.

Looking at certain facts one may be tempted to say that this end to the story is even probable. The Scots lost their political identity, their statehood, a quarter of a millenium ago. In our day they have pretty well lost the practical economic autonomy which succeeded it. The population has ceased to grow in numbers, though the birth rate is still high enough to make growth possible. The national system of education, which has helped to hold Scotsmen together, is weakening. In a sense the voice of Scotland is weakening too, since many of the newspapers and the radio are not under Scottish control.

There are some striking facts on the other side. In our day the administration of Scottish affairs in Scotland has developed in a surprising way: it may almost be said that the framework of a state exists again. The national Church, which has a quite remarkable place in Scottish life and history, has reunited and strengthened itself. Though it had never ceased to exist, national feeling has become much more self-conscious than it had been for several generations. It has expressed itself in politics but more effectively (as yet) in a rebirth of Scottish letters and in the growth of new institutions.

Short of a world-wide catastrophe, the future of Scotland depends entirely on the Scottish people themselves. Just as it is the sheer will to exist as a nation which keeps 4,750,000 Swiss (very prosperously) in the mountainous core of Europe, it is will rather than mere economic opportunity which has made Scotland and still holds even 5,000,000 Scots there. Certainly Scotland has economic resources, some of them undeveloped, but they do not lie on the surface, and if the wish to remain part of a Scottish community disappeared a good many of the 5,000,000 would probably find their way elsewhere. One or two depressed and dwindling cities apart, the country would be a rather rainy playground for Englishmen.

In a sense Scots who remain in Scotland have long been volunteers: the old tradition of emigration has made it easy and natural for them to choose where they would live. Consciously or unconsciously many of them are ready to pay something for the right to be in their own land—to work rather harder than some of their neighbours, to earn a little less, to bear taxation a good deal heavier than that of most small countries and see very little return at home for a good part of it. The spirit of public life in Scotland has always been a voluntary one. In the past Scots Governments were often too weak to control the unwilling. At present Scottish institutions, from the Church to bodies like the Scottish Council, could not exist without the unpaid work of many of those concerned with them.

In such conditions, if the will to keep the Scottish way of life going weakens everything else must go with it. A system of this sort can scarcely stand still. Those who belong to it must find new ways of expressing themselves, of meeting their own needs, of regaining what has been lost to them—in fact, of being effectively Scottish. Without this the system itself must die, and Scotland with it.

DATES AND EVENTS IN SCOTTISH HISTORY

Doubtful or traditional dates are italicized

A.D.

80	Romans in the Lowlands under Agricola.
84	Battle of Mons Graupius. Agricola defeats Caledonians. Lowlands held by Romans for twenty (?) years.
142–185	Antonine Wall, from Forth to Clyde, held by Romans.
197	Caledonians raid as far as York.
208	Emperor Severus reaches the Moray Firth.
360–8	Picts and Scots raid the Roman province of Britain, reaching London.
396	St. Ninian builds the church of Candida Casa (Whithorn).
495	Fergus Mor macErc, first King of the Scottish (Irish Gaelic) colony of Dalriada (in Argyllshire).
547	Ida, first king of the Anglic Kingdom of Bernicia (Northumberland and Lothian).
563	St. Columba, exiled from Ireland, settles in Iona.
565	The King of the Picts accepts Christianity.
573	Battle of Arderydd. Welsh Kingdom of Strathclyde consolidated.
654	Oswiu, King of Northumbria, supreme in North Britain.
685	Battle of Nectansmere. Brude mac Bili, King of the Picts, defeats and kills Ecgfrid, King of Northumbria. End of Anglic predominance.
732	Relics of the apostle Andrew said to have been brought to Kilrymont in Pictland, now St. Andrews.

795	First Norse raid on Iona.
836–918	Norse invasions.
844	Kenneth MacAlpin, King of the Scots in Argyllshire, becomes King of the Picts. His descendants have since ruled almost continuously.
867	Norse capture of York shatters Northumbrian Kingdom. Way opened for Picto-Scottish absorption of Lothian.
Before 900	Norse Jarldom of Orkney established in islands previously Pictish.
975 (about)	Conquest of Lothian by Kenneth II.
1018	Battle of Carham. Malcolm II, King of Scots, establishes frontier on the Tweed. Death of last King of Strathclyde, which till 1152 is normally held by Scots King's heir.
1040	Duncan I, King of Scots, defeated by Earl of Orkney. Revolt of Macbeth, ruler of Moray, who reigns as King of Scots till 1157.
1069	Malcolm III (Canmore), King of Scots, marries (St.) Margaret, sister of Edgar Atheling, heir of Saxon Kings of England, who has fled from William the Conqueror.
1070–93	Wars with Norman England. Malcolm III submits twice (to William I and William II). Scots expelled from Cumberland.
1102	Western Isles, already largely Norse, formally surrendered to Magnus Barefoot, King of Norway.
1124–52	David I, King of Scots (previously ruler of Strathclyde, where he had settled Norman barons), systematizes feudalism, founds bishoprics and abbeys, establishes burghs and shires.
1157	Scots claims to Northumberland and Cumberland abandoned.

1174	William I (the Lyon), King of Scots, captured on invasion of England, becomes vassal of Henry II, King of England, for Scotland, and receives English garrisons in Border castles.
1188	Church in Scotland declared directly subject to the Holy See by Pope Clement III.
1189	William I buys back his independence from Richard Coeur-de-Lion.
1263–6	Haakon the Old, King of Norway, attempts to re-establish his power in the Hebrides. Battle of Largs. Death of Haakon. Hebrides ceded to Scotland.
1286	Death of Alexander III, King of Scots, whose heiress is a grand-daughter, Margaret, infant daughter of the King of Norway.
1290	Treaty of Birgham for marriage of Margaret with Edward, Prince of Wales, son of Edward I of England, the laws and separate existence of Scotland to be maintained. Queen Margaret dies in Orkney.
1291–2	Edward I claims overlordship of Scotland, and chooses a vassal king, John Balliol, from thirteen competitors, one of them Robert Bruce (the elder).
1294	John Balliol refuses to join Edward in war with France. Scottish treaty with France: beginning of 'the Auld Alliance'.
1296	Battle of Dunbar. Scots defeated. John Balliol resigns kingdom to Edward I.
1297–8	Rising of William Wallace and Andrew Moray. English defeated at Stirling Bridge. Wallace, Guardian of the Kingdom, overcome by Edward I at Falkirk.
1299	New guardians of Scotland include Robert Bruce, grandson of the competitor.
1305	Capture and execution of Wallace. English conquest of Scotland complete.

1306–7	Rising of Robert Bruce. Crowned King of Scots. Defeated and leaves Scotland, but returns. Death of Edward I.
1314	Battle of Bannockburn. Decisive victory over Edward II of England.
1320	Arbroath Declaration of Scottish Independence addressed to the Pope.
1326	Scottish burghs join in a parliamentary grant of taxation.
1328	Treaty of Northampton. England admits complete independence of Scotland and recognizes Robert I (Bruce) as King.
1332–56	Wars as a result of English attempts to displace David II, son of Robert I.
1371	Robert II, grandson of Robert I, first Stewart King.
1406–24	James I, King of Scots, prisoner in England—he had been captured on his way to France at the age of eleven.
1411	University of St. Andrews founded.
1420	Scots expedition to aid French against Henry V of England.
1424–37	James I's reforms—legal aid, new supreme court, attempted organization of a House of Commons on English pattern (abortive), peerage (Lords of Parliament) established.
1437	James I murdered at Perth. His son, James II, aged six, King of Scots.
1469	James III receives Orkney in pledge for the dowry of his bride, Margaret of Denmark.
1472	St. Andrews made first Scottish archbishopric.
1488–1513	James IV, King of Scots. Age of the *Makaris*.
1503	James IV marries Margaret Tudor, daughter of Henry VII of England—origin of Stewart claim to the English crown.
1511–13	Holy League unites the Pope, Emperor,

England, Spain and Venice against France. Scots alliance with France confirmed. English claim to overlordship of Scotland revived. Henry VIII invades France. James IV invades England. Battle of Flodden. James IV defeated and killed. James V, aged one, King of Scots.

1528	Patrick Hamilton, Abbot of Fearn, a Lutheran and the King's cousin, burnt for heresy.
1532	College of Justice founded.
1542	War with England. Scots routed at Solway Moss. Death of James V. His daughter Mary, aged six days, Queen of Scots.
1543	Treaty of Greenwich for marriage of Mary with Edward, Prince of Wales. Scotland to remain separate kingdom.
1544–50	'The English Wooing'—wars to enforce the treaty, denounced by the Scots.
1546	George Wishart, Lutheran preacher, burnt for heresy at St. Andrews. Cardinal Beaton, Archbishop of St. Andrews, murdered by Protestants in revenge. John Knox preaches at St. Andrews.
1547	French troops aid Scottish Government.
1548	Mary Queen of Scots sent to France under arrangement for her marriage with the Dauphin.
1557	'Lords of the Congregation' make an agreement to establish Protestantism.
1559	War of the Congregation.
1560	Alliance between Lords of the Congregation and Elizabeth of England. Treaty of Edinburgh. French troops withdrawn, leaving Protestants in power. Parliament establishes Protestantism without the consent of Queen Mary and her husband, Francis II, King of France.

1561   Queen Mary returns widowed to Scotland.

1565   Mary marries Henry Stewart, Lord Darnley, whose mother stood next to herself among the heirs of Henry VII of England, while his father claimed to be heir-presumptive in Scotland. The Chaseabout Raid—Protestant rebels driven into England.

1566   Murder of David Rizzio, the Queen's secretary, by Darnley and Protestant Lords. Mary recovers power.

1567   Murder of Darnley. Mary abducted by Earl of Bothwell (probably one of his murderers), marries him. Forced to abdicate. James VI, her son, aged one, proclaimed King of Scots.

1568   Battle of Langside. Mary flees to England.

1571   Introduction of Protestant bishops.

1578   Second *Buke of Discipline* accepted by General Assembly. Bishops disavowed.

1581   Formal organization of presbyteries by General Assembly.

1587   Mary Queen of Scots executed in England.

1592   Act of Parliament establishing presbyterian government of the Church.

1603   Death of Queen Elizabeth of England. James VI, King of Scots, becomes King of England and Ireland.

1606   Act anent Colliers and Salters, establishing a form of serfdom in these trades.

1606–10 Re-establishment of the powers of bishops in the Kirk.

1610   Plantation of Ulster. Many Scots and English settled on confiscated Irish lands.

1625   Death of James VI and I. To provide for the Scottish Church, Charles I revokes grants of Church lands made since the Reformation.

1637   Scottish Book of Common Prayer imposed on the Kirk by royal command. Riot at St. Giles,

	Edinburgh. Commissions of lords, lairds, burgesses and ministers—'the Tables'—formed to protect the Kirk.
1638	The National Covenant. General Assembly at Glasgow deposes bishops.
1639–40	The Bishops' Wars. The Scots occupy Newcastle-on-Tyne. Charles I accepts revolutionary Acts of Parliament restoring Presbyterianism and giving Parliament control of the executive.
1641	Charles I visits Scotland to seek help against his English Parliament, in vain.
1643	Alliance between the Scottish and English Parliaments—the Solemn League and Covenant—for Reformation in a Presbyterian sense.
1644	Battle of Marston Moor. Victory of English and Scottish Parliamentary armies.
1644 (Sept.)–1645 (Sept.)	Marquis of Montrose, ex-covenanter and constitutional royalist, with a mainly Highland and Irish army, defeats the Covenanting forces in six battles but is crushed at Philiphaugh.
1646	Charles I gives himself up to Scots Covenanting army in England.
1647	King Charles handed over to English Parliamentary Army. The Engagement (agreement with Scots commissioners to confirm Presbyterianism in Scotland and give it a three years' trial in England) signed by the King at Carisbrooke.
1648	Scots army invades England and is defeated at Preston.
1649	Execution of Charles I in London. Charles II proclaimed King of Scots.
1650	Charles II takes the Covenant and comes to Scotland. Battle of Dunbar—Scots defeated by Oliver Cromwell.

1651	Charles II with Scots Army invades England. Defeated at Worcester.
1652	Scotland completely occupied.
1654	England, Scotland and Ireland united in one Commonwealth. Thirty Scots in joint Parliament.
1660–1	Restoration of Charles II. Union dissolved. General Act Recissory repeals all laws since 1638. Act for Erecting of Manufactories.
1662	Bishops restored to Parliament. Act requiring presentation and episcopal collation of ministers deprives 270 of their livings.
1666	First rising of Western Covenanters.
1679	Archbishop Sharp of St. Andrews murdered. Second rising of Covenanters defeated at Bothwell Bridge.
1681–6	The Killing Time—pursuit of Covenanting rebels.
1687	Indulgence of James VII and II offering freedom of worship to Presbyterians and Roman Catholics.
1688–9	William, Prince of Orange, nephew of James VII and II and husband of his elder daughter, invades England. James flees to France—Convention of Scots Estates declares that he has forfeited the Crown. Claim of Right, asserting freedom of Parliament and of burghs, and condemning prelacy. William II and Mary II elected King and Queen of Scots. First Jacobite rising collapses after victory at Killiecrankie.
1690	Presbyterianism re-established. Abolition of patronage.
1692	Massacre of Glencoe.
1695	Acts for establishing the Company of Scotland trading to Africa and the Indies, and the Bank of Scotland.

1696	Act for Settling of Schools.
1698–1700	Company of Scotland's effort to found a colony at Darien fails.
1702	Anne, Queen of Scots. Commissioners for a Union appointed in England and Scotland.
1703	Last Scottish Parliament elected. Act anent War and Peace, denying future sovereigns the right to make war or treaties. Union negotiation broken off.
1705	New Commission of Union.
1707	Act for securing the Protestant Religion and Presbyterian Church government. Act and Treaty of Union. Scottish representatives join Parliament in London.
1712	Patronage re-imposed on Kirk.
1715–16	Jacobite Rising. The Pretender, 'James VIII', comes to Scotland but leaves as rising collapses.
1718	First Glasgow-owned ship in tobacco trade.
1723	Formation of the Honourable Society of Improvers in the Knowledge of Agriculture.
1727	Board of Trustees for Manufacturers established to apply funds due to Scotland under the Union.
1734	First secession from Church of Scotland.
1745–6	Prince Charles Edward Stewart (grandson of James VII) lands in Moidart. Occupies Edinburgh. Victory at Prestonpans. Enters England. Retreats from Derby. Victory at Falkirk. Crushed at Culloden. Secretary of State for Scotland dismissed and not replaced.
1747	Abolition of heritable (feudal) justifications. Disarming Act forbids Highland dress.
1759	Carron Ironworks founded.
1761	Second Secession—the Relief Presbytery
1760s onwards.	Sheep farming introduced in Highlands.

1765	James Watt invents separate condenser for steam engine.
1768	Work on Forth and Clyde Canal begins.
1773–93	Clearances on Glengarry estates.
1775	Serfdom of colliers and salters relieved.
1776	Collapse of tobacco trade owing to American Revolution. Adam Smith's *Wealth of Nations* published.
1779	First cotton mill established.
1782	Cotton weavers form trade union.
1787	Delegates of fifty-four towns prepare scheme for burgh reform.
1793	Thomas Muir and others sentenced for advocating constitutional reform.
1802	Steamer *Charlotte Dundas* on Forth and Clyde Canal.
1807	Fishery Board for Scotland established.
1811–20	Sutherland clearances.
1812	Steamer *Comet* on Clyde.
1820	'Radical Rising.' Leaders executed.
1832	Parliamentary Reform Act. Kirkintilloch Railway worked by steam.
1834	Scottish Burgh Reform Act—elected town councils.
1843	Disruption of the Church of Scotland. Free Church of Scotland formed.
1845	Parochial Boards and central Board of Supervision to control poor relief.
1846	Highland potato famine.
1847	United Presbyterian Church founded by union of Relief and United Secession Churches.
1853	Scottish Rights Association, for redress of political grievances.
1871	Steel Company of Scotland established.
1872	Scottish Education Act. Compulsory education. School boards and central Scotch Education Department.

1874	Patronage in Church of Scotland abolished by Parliament. Collapse of wool prices: spread of deer forests.
1877	First steel ships built on Clyde.
1883 onwards.	Crofter no-rent campaign.
1885	Office of Secretary for Scotland established.
1886	Crofters' Holdings Act gives security of tenure. Scottish Home Rule Association founded.
1888	Scottish Labour Party founded—for land nationalization, eight-hour day, Home Rule, etc.
1889	County councils established.
1894	Standing Committee on Scottish Bills formed in House of Commons.
1895	Parish Councils succeed parochial boards.
1900	Local Government Board for Scotland (Department of Health after 1928). United Free Church of Scotland formed by Free Church and United Presbyterians.
1912	Board of Agriculture for Scotland (Department of Agriculture after 1928). Scottish Land Court.
1914–18	World War.
1918	National Bank of Scotland acquired by Lloyd's Bank—others followed.
1921	Railways Act. Scottish lines merged with English.
1926	Secretary for Scotland becomes Secretary of State.
1928	National Party of Scotland founded.
1929	Union of Church of Scotland with United Free Church. Local Government (Scotland) Act—parish councils abolished. City and county councils take over education, poor relief.

1931	Scottish National Development Council founded.
1939	Re-organization of Offices (Scotland) Act. Secretary of State takes direct control of all Scottish Departments. Home Department founded.
1939–45	World War.
1943	North of Scotland Hydro-Electric Board formed.
1946–8	Nationalization (for the United Kingdom) of coal, railways and other transport, electricity, gas, medical services, poor relief.
1949	Scottish Covenant campaign launched.
1951	Minister of State, Scottish Office, appointed.
1955	Crofters' Commission established.

SOME SCOTTISH BOOKS

This is far from being a complete list of books on subjects touched on in the present volume. It is intended simply to help readers who may look for further information.

General Works

There are no modern books of an encyclopaedic character dealing only or mainly with Scottish subjects, except the *Encyclopaedia of the Laws of Scotland*, 18 vols., a useful reference work for many topics. Publications which range widely are *Scotland: A Description of Scotland and Scottish Life*, edited by H. W. Meikle (1947), with chapters of varying value on many aspects and activities; *Scotland* by Sir Robert Rait and George S. Pryde, 2nd edition (1954), containing useful information on events in this century besides earlier history; and *Scotland* by Ian Finlay (1957), a more personal view. One of the earliest works of its kind for any country, *The Statistical Account of Scotland*, 21 vols. (1791–9)—the 'Old Statistical'—was followed by *The New Statistical Account of Scotland*, 15 vols. (1845). Supplemented by the *Ordnance Gazetteer of Scotland*, 6 vols. (1882 onwards), these give a comprehensive view of the country in its first industrial periods and are now being followed by *The Third Statistical Account of Scotland* (1951 onwards), unfortunately, though perhaps inevitably, on a rather different plan. *Scotland: a Select Bibliography* (1950) is a useful short book list.

History

P. Hume Brown's *History of Scotland*, 3 vols. (1900–9), is still regarded as the standard work, though it has the limitations which might be expected in the writing of a late-Victorian Whig. Six volumes by Agnes Mure Mackenzie, *The Foundations of Scotland, Robert Bruce, King of Scots, The Rise of the Stewarts, The Scotland of Queen Mary and the Religious Wars, The Passing of the Stewarts* and *Scotland in Modern Times* (1934–41) present a revaluation of the record in the spirit of the Scottish Renaissance. They are summarized in one volume, in *The Kingdom of Scotland* (1940). *The Scots Tragedy* by Colin Walkinshaw (1935) gives a theory of Scottish history from a similar point of view. Other one-volume accounts are W. M. Mackenzie's *Outline of Scottish History* (1907), R. L. Mackie's *A Short History of Scotland* (1930) and G. M. Thomson's book of the same name (1932).

Though much criticized and badly in need of re-editing W. F. Skene's *Celtic Scotland*, 3 vols. (2nd edition 1886–90), is still the only comprehensive account of the early centuries. W. L. Matheson's four volumes, *Politics and Religion in Scotland, Scotland and the Union, The Awakening of Scotland* and *Church and Reform in Scotland* (1902–17) cover the development of Scottish opinion and its effects from the Reformation to the mid-Nineteenth Century. H. W. Meikle's *Scotland and the French Revolution* (1912) is indispensable for its period. For the traditional view and picturesque incidents Sir Walter Scott's *Tales of a Grandfather* (1828–30) can never be replaced. Useful extracts from the ancient historians and documents are in A. O. M. Anderson's *Early Sources of Scottish History*, 2 vols. (1922), and *Scottish Annals from English Chroniclers* (1908), *A Source Book of Scottish History*, edited by W. C. Dickinson and others (1952 onwards), J. G. Fyfe's *Scottish Diaries and Memoirs 1550–1843*, 2 vols. (1928–42), and Agnes Mure Mackenzie's colourful *Scottish Pageant*, 4 vols. (1946–50).

Economics

The Scottish Economy, edited by A. K. Cairncross 1954), gives a statistical account of various sides of

Scottish life, particularly useful on industry and population. Henry Hamilton's *The Industrial Revolution in Scotland* (1932) and I. F. Grant's *The Social and Economic Development of Scotland before 1603* (1930) and her short *Economic History of Scotland* (1934) are supplemented by W. H. Marwick's *Economic Developments in Victorian Scotland* (1936). *A History of Banking in Scotland* by A. W. Kerr (new edition, revised by F. H. Allan, 1926) and Thomas Johnston's *History of the Working Classes in Scotland* (1920) are well known. For the land, T. B. Franklin's *A History of Scottish Farming* (1952), Adam Collier's *The Crofting Problem* (1953), F. Fraser Darling's *West Highland Survey* (1955) and Malcolm Gray's *The Highland Economy 1750-1850* (1957).

The Church

Scottish church history still needs extensive rewriting. *The Church of Scotland from the Commencement of the Christian Era to the Present Time* by John Cunningham, 2 vols. (2nd edition 1882), is still perhaps the completest account, though much out of date. G. D. Henderson's *The Claims of the Church of Scotland* (1951) and *The Church of Scotland, A Short History* (1939) probably give the most informative sketch. *The Churches in Scotland Today* by John Highet (1950) is a useful statistical survey.

Education

There is no satisfying general account of Scottish education, either historical or topical. Histories are *Rise and Progress of Scottish Education* by A. Morgan (1927) and *Two Hundred and Fifty Years of Scottish Education* by H. M. Knox (1953). John Highet's chapter on Education in *The Scottish Economy* (above) fills a gap.

Law

For the layman the most illuminating discussion of Scots Law is probably to be found in *Selected Papers* by Lord Cooper of Culross (1957) which reprints his pamphlet on *The Scottish Legal Tradition*. A. D. Gibb's *A Preface to Scots Law* (1950) is a useful outline, and T. B. Smith's contribution on Scotland to *The British Commonwealth: the Development of its Laws and Contribution*, edited by G. W. Keston (Vol. I, 1955), a full analysis remarkable for its lucidity.

Government Politics, Administration

The growth of government is dealt with in general histories, but more particularly in *The Parliaments of Scotland* by R. S. Rait (1924), and *The Scottish Burghs* by W. M. Mackenzie (1949). Two brief accounts of *Local Government in Scotland* are by J. D. Mackie and G. S. Pryde (1936), and by J. E. Shaw (1942). The development of the Home Rule movement is dealt with in *Scottish Devolution* (1950) by W. H. Marwick and, with much more personal feeling, in *The Flag in the Wind* by J. M. MacCormick (1955). *Scottish Empire* by A. D. Gibb (1937) describes the contribution of Scotsmen to the growth of the British Empire. *The Scottish Office* by Sir David Milne (1958) gives a useful account of most of the work of government in Scotland from an official point of view.

The Arts

A fresh and often perceptive account of Scottish literary history is *The Scottish Tradition in Literature* by Kurt Wittig (1958). J. H. Millar's *A Literary History of Scotland* (1903) remains worth reading, as does *An Historical Survey of Scottish Literature to 1714* by Agnes Mure Mackenzie (1933). *Modern Scottish Literature* by J. M. Reid, a Saltire pamphlet (1945), deals with the

Nineteenth and Twentieth Centuries. *Scottish Poetry: a Critical Survey*, edited by James Kinsley (1955), is impressively intelligent and comprehensive. *A Scots Anthology from the Thirteenth to the Twentieth Century*, edited by J. W. Oliver and J. C. Smith (1949), *Modern Scottish Poetry*, edited by Maurice Lindsay (1946), and *Scottish Verse, 1851-1951*, edited by Douglas Young (1951), are important collections.

Ian Finlay's *Art in Scotland* (1948) gives a somewhat idiosyncratic view of the visual arts generally. Stanley Cursiter's *Scottish Art to the Close of the Nineteenth Century* (1949) concentrates on painting. *The Stones of Scotland*, edited by George Scott-Moncrieff (1938), and *Story of Scotland in Stone* by Ian C. Hannah (1934) are introductions to Scottish architectural history but both close with the Eighteenth Century. *The Scottish Tradition in Burgh Architecture* by Ian G. Lindsay (1948) is a stimulating summary. *The Architecture of Scottish Post-Reformation Churches* by George Hay (1957) is original, learned and readable but ends in the mid-Nineteenth Century.

INDEX

PRINTED AT THE RIVERSIDE PRESS, EDINBURGH